CLASS WAR?

CLASS

BENJAMIN I. PAGE

LAWRENCE R. JACOBS

The University of Chicago Press

WAR?

What Americans Really Think
about Economic Inequality

CHICAGO & LONDON

BENJAMIN I. PAGE

is the Gordon Scott Fulcher Professor of Decision Making in the Department of Political Science at Northwestern University and is an
associate of the Institute for Policy Research.

LAWRENCE R. JACOBS

is the Walter F. and Joan Mondale Chair for Political Studies and di-
rector of the Center for the Study of Politics and Governance at the
Hubert H. Humphrey Institute of Public Affairs at the University of
Minnesota. He is also professor in the Department of Political Science.

The University of Chicago Press, Chicago 60637
The University of Chicago Press, Ltd., London
© 2009 by The University of Chicago
All rights reserved. Published 2009
Printed in the United States of America
18 17 16 15 14 13 12 11   2 3 4 5

ISBN-13: 978-0-226-64454-7 (cloth)
ISBN-13: 978-0-226-64455-4 (paper)
ISBN-10: 0-226-64454-5 (cloth)
ISBN-10: 0-226-64455-3 (paper)

Library of Congress Cataloging-in-Publication Data
Page, Benjamin I.
Class war? : what Americans really think about economic inequality /
Benjamin I. Page, Lawrence R. Jacobs.
p. cm.
Includes bibliographical references and index.
ISBN-13: 978-0-226-64454-7 (cloth : alk. paper)
ISBN-13: 978-0-226-64455-4 (pbk. : alk. paper)
ISBN-10: 0-226-64454-5 (cloth : alk. paper)
ISBN-10: 0-226-64455-3 (pbk. : alk. paper)   1. Income distribution—
United States—Public opinion.   2. Public opinion—United States.
3. United States—Economic conditions.   4. United States—Social
conditions.   5. United States—Politics and government.
I. Jacobs, Lawrence R.   II. Title.
HC110 .I5P344 2009   339.2′20973—dc22
2008043595

For Mary and Julie

Contents

Preface

While some have prospered beyond imagination in this global economy, middle-class Americans—as well as those working hard to become middle class—are seeing the American dream slip further and further away. BARACK OBAMA[1]

After the election of President Obama and large Democratic congressional majorities in 2008, it was natural to wonder what would become of their proposals to shift resources toward middle-class and working-class people. Would most Americans embrace such policies? Or would they reject them as inciting "class warfare"? What do Americans really think about economic inequality? How well or badly will politicians respond to their wishes?

Class conflict has never been completely absent from the United States. At some points in the past America has witnessed pitched battles at picket lines and factory gates. Yet these battles have generally lacked the broader public and political expressions found in Europe.

Various explanations have been offered for America's comparatively muted class conflict: the nature of our class structure (heavily middle class), our ethnically and racially divided working class, our abundant natural resources and economic opportunities, or the absence of a feudal past to revolt against.

The sharp and rapid increases in economic inequality that we have experienced since the 1970s—with wage stagnation or decline for most Americans accompanied by enormous gains for top income earners—might have been expected to ignite class warfare. Instead, widening inequality coincided with the further decline of organized labor, a political drift toward the Republican Party, and (at times) a bipartisan embrace of conservative policy approaches that rely on private markets instead of government.

Today's muted class divide might be thought to be a result of to Americans not being aware of or particularly concerned about economic inequality. After all, although disparities in the distribution of income and wealth have widened, most Americans still enjoy comforts that are the envy of other parts of the world, from ownership of homes and automobiles, to vacation travel, and to entertainment by a multitude of electronic gadgets. Large majorities of Americans might be expected to accept inequality in the belief that it is their ticket to pursue the American Dream for themselves or their kids. "Bill Gates can have his fortune as long as we get our shot at winning the jackpot."

Even if Americans knew about widening economic disparities and were agitated about them, one might imagine that they lack enthusiasm for potential remedies in terms of government policies. Past survey research has documented the generally conservative inclination of Americans to back individual opportunity, support free enterprise, be suspicious of government, and oppose taxes.

This book draws upon a warehouse of data, however, to demonstrate that today most of these expectations are not actually borne out. Most Americans *are* aware of high and increasing economic inequality. Most are unhappy about it. Most favor a wide range of concrete, pragmatic government programs when their well-being is threatened or opportunity is blocked by forces beyond their control.

Most are willing to pay taxes to foot the bill. In terms of public support, the prospects for egalitarian policy changes would seem to be bright—though politicians' responsiveness may be another matter.

An important reason for the lack of class war is actually widespread *agreement* across social and economic classes in favor of targeted government programs that foster the American Dream and provide a measure of economic security. What is startling is that this agreement is based on a rejection—not an ignoring, let alone an embrace—of today's wide and growing disparities in income and wealth. Majorities of Republicans as well as Democrats, and majorities of high-income earners as well as those of middle and low income, recognize the growth of extreme economic inequality, object to it, and favor government remedies supported by tax dollars. Even affluent Americans are concerned about inequality and are willing to make personal sacrifices to deal with it.

Our careful exploration of the data leads to a fascinating and perhaps counterintuitive picture of America that defies simple bifurcation into conservative and liberal camps. The evidence shows that most Americans are *both* philosophically conservative and operationally liberal. They believe in the American Dream, individual initiative, and free markets. In the abstract, they are uneasy with government. But Americans are also pragmatic. When their well-being (and that of people they care about) is threatened, or when their dreams are blocked by forces beyond their control, they turn to concrete government programs for help—programs that would greatly decrease economic inequality. Most Americans are *conservative egalitarians*.

This conclusion raises unsettling questions about why pundits and policy makers are often so far off the mark. Why so many talking heads insist on ignoring the wide areas of agreement among Americans, and instead hype the differences? Why have elected government officials often failed to respond to the large majorities within both parties and all income groups that agree in favoring many pragmatic egalitarian policies?

This is an unusual book to come from a university press. It is chiefly aimed at a broad audience of general readers, not just scholarly experts and students of American politics, inequality, public opinion, and the like (though it has plenty to say to them, too). For that reason we have forsaken some of the conventions of academia, in the hope of communicating with general readers who might be put off by scholarly jargon. We do make references, in endnotes and occasionally in the text, to particularly important past research. And we do at times flag significant disputes over what the facts are or how they should be interpreted. But we do this less than is usual in scholarly books or articles. For readers interested in delving into the details of scholarly debates, we encourage them to track down the citations we provide and we welcome them to consider our own writings published elsewhere, including the report from an authoritative task force concerning inequality and American democracy that was convened by the American Political Science Association.[2]

We have deliberately set out to write a different kind of book than we have written in the past, a book with clear implications for policy making. We decided not to focus primarily on identifying areas of scholarly debate and then staking out our own position. Instead, we enter the broad realm of public discourse. We quote and discuss the views of TV commentators, newspaper columnists, government officials, and others involved in the practicalities of making public policy. We also include the voices of many everyday Americans, through their letters to the editors of newspapers around the United States and their comments as captured in news stories from their communities. While some academics may be surprised by this material, our hope is that most readers will find that it makes the discussion more approachable and engaging.

Even as we have written for a broad audience, this book rests on a vast body of meticulous research concerning public opinion. It makes use of our own new, uniquely comprehensive opinion survey—the Inequality Survey—as well as an exhaustive review of decades' worth of previous surveys. In our own survey we asked many questions (preserving identical question wording) drawn from previous surveys—some of which date back to the 1930s. This allows us to situate our findings in the context of past public attitudes. It enables us to identify changes over time and to compare our findings with those from previous research. We confirm, update, or (in some cases) refute virtually all the main conclusions of previous researchers. The details about this are relegated to endnotes; only major continuities and changes are mentioned in the text.

In short, this book rests on literally hundreds of opinion surveys conducted since the 1930s. In addition to presenting some startling new findings, it confirms and updates a number of long-established patterns that are broadly accepted by all serious students of American public opinion.

Our aim has been to write a book that is relevant to our time *and* meets rigorous scholarly standards. We embrace an old and honorable tradition in the social sciences, that of engaged scholarship. We speak not only to scholars and students but also to the broader political world in the hope that we may have some modest impact on the shape of public policy in the future.

We are grateful to Melanie Burns for her remarkable energy, patience, and expert research skills. We are also grateful for the feedback and suggestions of Andrea Campbell, Tom Ferguson, Dan Galvin, Ed Greenberg, Lane Kenworthy, Leslie McCall, Suzanne Mettler, Ben R. Page, and two anonymous reviewers. Sam Best and his colleagues at the University of Connecticut's Center for Survey Research and Analysis deserve recognition for their helpful and valued work in fielding our survey. We remain responsible for the evidence and interpretations reported here.

BENJAMIN I. PAGE
LAWRENCE R. JACOBS

1

No Class War

We have to do something about the extraordinary economic inequality . . .
the worst it's been since the Great Depression.   JOHN EDWARDS[1]

[R]ising inequality . . . has been evident for at least three decades. . . . [N]o
one should be allowed to slip too far down the economic ladder, especially
for reasons beyond his or her control.   BEN BERNANKE[2]

[I]ncome inequality is real [and has] been rising for more than twenty-five
years.   GEORGE W. BUSH[3]

In recent decades affluent Americans grew richer while the incomes
and assets of middle- and working-class Americans stagnated, and
then the economic crisis swamped all boats, leaving inequality high.
Observers from across the political spectrum—from liberal Democrats like John Edwards, to Barack Obama, to financial-establishment
figures like Federal Reserve chairman Ben Bernanke and Republicans
like George W. Bush—have flagged the widening gap between the
wealthy and other Americans as a problem.

But not everyone agrees, and policies to reduce inequality face potent challenges. Some say that inequality is actually good. Rewarding some much more than others, it is argued, is a necessary feature of market economies since it generates incentives for effort and investment. Why work hard and take risks if you can't reap more than the next person?

Some argue that the American public poses a particularly daunting barrier to addressing inequality. They assert that most ordinary Americans are uninterested in, or opposed to, reducing inequality. Others warn alarmingly of wide, deep, and potentially explosive divisions in the public. While Democrats and the less economically well-off may favor doing something about inequality, Republicans and the affluent are said to be intensely opposed. To try to do anything to reduce economic inequality would allegedly ignite "class warfare."

The research reported in this book should correct such misimpressions and quiet such fears. It shows that majorities of Americans—majorities of Republicans as well as Democrats, and majorities of the affluent as well as middle- and lower-income earners—see economic inequality in the United States as having become excessive. They favor certain government interventions to expand opportunity and the conditions to pursue it, and are willing to use their tax dollars to pay for such policies.

Agreement, not class war, is a striking, yet often-ignored, feature of public thinking about economic inequality. This widespread agreement across classes and parties is seldom mentioned by talking heads or politicians. Curiously, some elected officials ignore or oppose the views of large majorities of the public that they claim to represent, even the views of their fellow partisans.

While Americans are alert to inequality and support measures that would reduce it, however, they remain conservative by instinct and by philosophical inclination. More so than citizens in Germany, France, or other Western democracies, Americans favor the free-enterprise system and oppose extensive government interference in the economy. They also embrace the "American Dream"—the idea that individuals should enjoy the opportunity to go as far as their work and skill will take them. Responsibility for an individual's economic position and life conditions rests chiefly with him- or herself. Government is the object of widespread suspicion about ineffectiveness, waste, and corruption. These suspicions are widely shared, even among rank-and-file Democrats.

The pressing issue of health-care reform exemplifies the public's mix of attitudes. Proponents of moving in one fell swoop to a Single Payer health-care system can justifiably point to the pragmatic inclination of Americans to extend health insurance to all Americans, which would remove an important contributor to inequality. (Many hardworking people sink under medical bills or lose their jobs owing to treatable illnesses.) Yet Americans are keenly sensitive to any dramatic expansion of government, and they resist any perceived threat to their own personal choices or personal arrangements for medical care—arrangements that many value highly. This public unease with drastic changes, exploited by opponents of reform, has helped block comprehensive national health-insurance reform for more than a century.

Americans are both philosophically conservative *and* operationally liberal. They believe in individual responsibility, free enterprise, and the American Dream. This is a conservative view of the world, one that is buttressed by deep-seated suspicion and unease regarding the competence and integrity of government.

Yet Americans are also pragmatic in sizing up the actual operation of our society. They expect individuals to take care of themselves, but they accept that government help may be needed to address concrete barriers to pursuing opportunity. Americans favor programs that equip individuals to pursue employment opportunities through education and training, and programs that protect them from threats to economic security such as illness, old age, or disability.

America's unique blend of philosophical conservatism and operational liberalism leads to a particular approach to addressing economic inequality, an approach we can call *conservative egalitarianism.*

The American public's way of thinking about these matters is badly misunderstood. Political operatives and pundits go wrong when they insist on squeezing Americans into preconceived red/blue or liberal/ conservative categories that do not fit.

This book offers a fast-moving but thorough report on the state of public thinking about economic inequality and what (if anything) should be done about it. Rather than imposing preconceived views, we present the evidence from a mountain of research and follow where it leads. We have conducted our own new, uniquely comprehensive national opinion survey. We have also exhaustively examined many decades' worth of past surveys. Our own survey's use of previously asked survey questions—some dating back to the 1930s—makes it possible for us to report trends in public opinion over many years, incorporating and updating virtually all of the main findings by previous researchers. What we report reflects the collective findings of dozens of nonpartisan, independent survey analysts.

Even in the face of a mountain of evidence, reconsidering long-accepted assumptions can be hard and challenging work. It requires patience and a willingness to follow the evidence to its logical conclusion.

Here is our road map. We begin by briefly sketching the evidence from economists and statisticians about the actual distribution of income and wealth in the United States today. A broad (though not completely unanimous) array of experts and government officials has concluded that economic inequality has risen sharply, and see this as a serious problem. We then discuss the widespread assumption that Americans accept extreme economic inequality. We move on to present real-world evidence about public attitudes and perceptions that demolishes any such notion.

Widening Inequality

Bill Gates—the founder of the computer software company Microsoft—ranks among the wealthiest Americans of all time. His fortune in 2007 stood at about $82 billion. Some have calculated that he has hauled in $1 million per hour (that's $300 per second). If he dropped a $1,000 bill on his way to work, he could have lost money by stopping to pick it up.[4]

Put in the perspective of American history, Gates ranked with the wealthiest "robber barons" from a century ago. His net worth as a share of the economy made him the fifth wealthiest American ever, behind oil baron John D. Rockefeller and real-estate magnate John Jacob Astor, and just ahead of steel kingpin Andrew Carnegie.[5]

Gates is one of a small group of Americans whose income and wealth exploded while the economic standing of middle America stalled. Take a lesser-known example of today's super rich. Twenty-five managers of private businesses that invest money (known as "hedge funds") each took home a minimum of $240 million in 2006. The top salary was $1.7 billion. Added together, those twenty-five individuals were paid more than $14 billion—more than the entire gross domestic product of Jordan or Uruguay. They made enough to *double* the income of every one of the 3.5 million men, women, and children in Uruguay, or the 6 million in Jordan.[6]

Incredibly, hedge-fund managers did even better in 2007. The total take of the top twenty-five jumped from $14 billion to $22 billion (about equal to the GDP of Costa Rica and a third more than Iceland's).[7] The top five hedge-fund managers each took home more than $1 billion—that is, one thousand million dollars. John Paulson was champ at about $3.7 billion; George Soros placed second with roughly $2.9 billion; and James Simons, who had ranked first in 2006, dropped into third place with a mere $2.8 billion. No doubt it was some consolation to Simons that his income more than doubled from the previous year.[8]

The soaring fortunes of the super rich have remade the overall distribution of income and wealth in the United States. The evidence of widening inequality comes from nonpartisan economists and independent government offices like the Treasury Department, the Internal Revenue Service, and the Federal Reserve Board.

Three major changes have resliced America's economic pie.

A RECORD-BREAKING GAP IN TAKE-HOME PAY. First/ we made the record books as the take-home pay for the rich soared while it flattened out for middle America. After the mid-1970s, the real hourly wages for middle and lower income groups fell or stagnated, with one exception—the latter half of the 1990s, when full employment temporarily forced employers to offer higher wages to attract workers. But overall, real median family income—that is, the total income of the average family, in "real" (inflation-adjusted) dollars—declined by 3 percent. In 2004 dollars that comes out to a decline of $1,600 per family, not the steady rise envisioned in the American Dream. Meanwhile, high-income earners experienced sharp and nearly uninterrupted hikes for most of the past three decades.[9]

Stagnating or falling wages for low- and middle-wage earners, contrasting with the sharp increases for higher-income people, produced the largest gap in U.S. history. As economists Lawrence Mishel, Jared Bernstein, and Sylvia Allegretto observed, "[t]he very highest earners have done considerably better than other workers for at least 30 years, but they have done extraordinarily well over the last 10 years."[10] By 2005, the most affluent fifth received 48.1 percent of family income; the upper part of the middle class earned 15 or 20 percent, and the bottom two fifths each received less than 10 percent. Put simply, the richest 20 percent enjoyed nearly half of the country's income. Moreover, fully 21 percent of family income went to the top 5 percent of Americans, a very fortunate group indeed.

The sharply widening gap between the rich and everyone else is particularly striking because it persisted even during upbeat economic conditions, when a rising tide is supposed to "lift all boats." The economy has grown, and there has been a historic transformation in productivity (the output of goods and services per hour worked). The introduction and efficient use of information technology associated with computers and new software fuelled a take-off in productivity: it shot up from an average 1.4 percent improvement per year between the 1970s and mid-1990s, to 2.5 percent per year increases between 1995 and 2000, to a remarkable 3.1 percent annual improvement, on the average, between 2000 and 2005.[11] But these gains have not been shared with the workers who made them.

THE MOST GOES TO THE VERY RICHEST. The second change is that the very richest Americans do by far the best. Among the rich, $5 or $10 million barely registers. A Silicon Valley pioneer in creating online technology candidly noted that "You're nobody here at $10 million." In the world of the rich, there's a race for more and more wealth—as one humble owner of $5 million explains, "the top 1 percent chases the top one-tenth of 1 percent, and the top one-tenth of 1 percent chases the top one-one hundredth of 1 percent."[12]

This frantic sprint by the super rich pays off. From 1979 to 2000, the real income of families in the bottom fifth grew by about 6 percent and the middle fifth rose 12 percent. Meanwhile, the income of the top fifth increased 70 percent, and the take of those in the top 1 percent of households exploded by a staggering 184 percent. In 2004, the top 1 percent received over 16 percent of all the income in the country, while the rest of those in the top 10 percent got 9 percent of it.[13] The 90 percent of Americans with lower incomes were left far behind. Figure 1.1 shows that the tilt toward the very top income earners has sharply increased since the mid-1970s and became comparable to the extreme inequality of the 1920s.[14]

This sharp increase in inequality has been tracked by economists using the "Gini coefficient." A Gini coefficient of zero represents perfect equality (where each person has exactly the same income), and 1.0 signifies perfect inequality (where one person in a huge population has all the income—no one else has any). Like the Richter scale that measures the magnitude of earthquakes, the Gini coefficient lets us make comparisons over time. For family incomes, the Gini coefficient reached its highest level in six decades. The coefficient rose by about one quarter since 1947.[15]

THE GAP IN WEALTH IS LARGER STILL. The third big development is that the deluge of money toward the top is actually smaller in terms of take-home pay than it is for *wealth*: for property and assets,

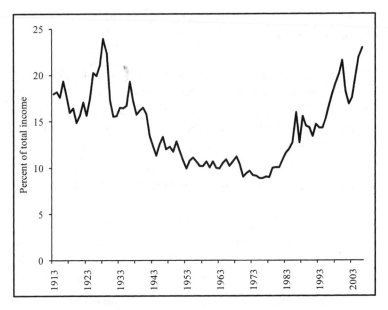

FIGURE 1.1 Concentration of income accruing to top 1 percent of families, 1913–2006. Source: Data from Piketty and Saez (2003), series updated to 2006. Income is defined as market income including capital gains. Top 1 percent denotes the top percentile (families with annual income above $382,600 in 2006).

including everything from real estate and fine art to stock market investments. A survey of consumer finances conducted by the authoritative Federal Reserve Board in 2004 revealed the distribution of household income and net worth (i.e., total family assets minus liabilities such as mortgages and other forms of debt). The top 1 percent of households drew about 17 percent of all income but wielded control over double this proportion of the country's wealth (34 percent). By contrast, the supermajority of the country—the "bottom" 90 percent of households—earned the majority of household income (57.5 percent) but controlled only 29 percent of the country's wealth.[16] This and other evidence shows that the vast majority of Americans enjoy very little of the country's wealth while a tiny proportion control an enormous share. Most of that represents huge gains on the stock market, where a tiny fraction of Americans own most of the shares.[17]

The concentration of wealth is especially extreme at the very pinnacle of the distribution. In 2000 (according to estate-tax data, which tend to underestimate inequality) the average member of the top 1/100th of 1 percent of wealth holders—with $63,564,000 or more—had about 463 times as much wealth as the average member of the bottom 90 percent of the population. And the top 101 wealth holders—with more than $8 billion each—averaged an astounding 59,619 times as much wealth as the average member of the bottom 90 percent of the population.[18]

Little wonder that economist Edward Wolff refers to the distribution of wealth in the United States as "top heavy."[19] The story line is simple: the distribution of income has become far more concentrated since the 1970s, and the concentration of wealth is even more extreme.

Inequality has always existed in America, and very few observers are suggesting that it is about to disappear or that it should be completely eliminated. The issue is that over the past three decades, the share taken by the rich and the super rich soared to a far higher level than at any time since the highly unequal 1920s or the Gilded Age of the 1890s. One review observed: "Only twice before over the last century has 5 percent of the national income gone to families in the upper one-one-hundredth of one percent of the income distribution—currently, the roughly 15,000 families with incomes of $9.5 million or more a year."[20]

What kind of society have we become? Recently a newspaper reporter visited Fisher Island—a Florida paradise framed by Miami Beach, Miami, Biscayne Bay, and the Atlantic Ocean. The ferry to the island conspicuously displayed the contrasts in today's America, between "[r]ich people, many in expensive cars, and servants, who board on foot and take their spots on benches."[21] In Florida and elsewhere, Barbara Ehrenreich has chronicled the struggles of waiters, house cleaners, and others—often without health insurance, reliable transportation, or decent shelter—who cater to the affluent.[22]

DISPUTES ABOUT INEQUALITY. The basic facts about economic inequality are rock solid. The statistics have been meticulously gathered and analyzed by nonpartisan economists, respected government agencies, and independent bodies that work closely with Wall Street firms and private bankers and investors.

Although the facts are clear, at least five disputes have developed over how to interpret and react to them. The first dispute focuses on the use of "averages." Columnist David Brooks, for example, dismisses what he calls "incredibly simple minded" accounts of inequality by hailing the "complicating fact" that "average wages are rising sharply."[23] Brooks's statement about average (mean) wages has been correct, at least before the current downturn. But it is not relevant to questions about inequality, which concern dispersions or differences—not averages. And a focus on means can overstate the welfare of the typical person. Bill Gates can walk into a slum full of the poorest people in Calcutta, or into a middle-class dinner club in Mount Vernon, Iowa, and immediately send the mean ("average") income and wealth skyrocketing without actually improving the situation of anyone else. President Bush, Federal Reserve Chairman Bernanke, and many economists focus on what is happening to individuals or families in the middle compared to the super rich, not what is happening to the average of everybody added together.[24]

A second kind of dispute about inequality focuses on what to count. Some discussions of inequality concentrate on assets without considering the distribution of *net* wealth or net income. Columnist Bill Kristol, for example, challenges the importance of statistics on wealth inequality by pointing to the number of Americans who own their homes, neglecting to consider the loans and debt burdens incurred—a reality made dramatically clear by the recent mortgage crisis and the epidemic of foreclosures.[25] A related issue is raised by Alan Reynolds at the Cato Institute, who challenges the dependence of some researchers on federal income tax returns. The problem, Reynolds maintains, is that findings of increased inequality merely reflect changes in tax rules, not actual changes in income.[26] In reality, however, broadly similar findings about over-time change have been reported using a range of data, including those collected by the U.S. Census Bureau.

A third dispute involves the reasonable point that measured inequality may partly reflect temporary fluctuations or gradual changes over people's life cycles. Some of us start out with minimum-wage jobs as kids and then move up the occupational ladder to well-paying positions. While inequality across individuals at one point in time looks very large, we might find less of a gap in the *lifetime incomes* of different individuals. Michael Cox has argued that it is "not a wage gap but an age gap."[27] But research using panel data on the same individuals over time finds persistent inequality in lifetime earnings as well. One study, for instance, followed the same low-income people from childhood into early adulthood and found that just over half of white children and three-quarters of black children remained mired in the poorest fifth of income earners or at best moved up to the second-poorest fifth.[28] Research tracking families yields no more encouraging results: fewer than 5 percent of families moved from the poorest to the richest quintile during the 1970s, 1980s, and 1990s. About half of those in the middle quintile moved up or down a fifth, and what movement did occur slowed down in later years.[29]

A fourth, but related, dispute about inequality concerns the assertion that America is a remarkably mobile society. Inequality may be wide today, it is said, but that does not matter much because the American Dream creates an economic escalator that allows the poor and middle-class people—or their children—to move up while those at the top move down. This is a rousing tale, made believable by stories of remarkable individuals who have overcome hardships and long odds to rise to the top. But research by Peter Gottschalk and other economists—while carefully highlighting complications related to conceptualization and measurement—finds little evidence to support the hopeful belief that those at the bottom can consistently work their way up. A few Americans do make it from the bottom to the top, but this is rare. The economic positions of parents have a large and enduring impact on their children's later economic positions. It is hard to escape the general rule that it matters more to whom you are born than what you do.[30]

Indeed, research shows that the rich and super rich are so ensconced at the top of American society that European economies, supposedly weighted down by aristocratic traditions and large welfare states, may now offer *greater* upward mobility than the United States does. Even the cautious head of America's central bank acknowledges evidence that upward mobility in America fails to offset inequality.[31]

A fifth dispute concerns the claim that most Americans care about what they have—which is a lot—not about how much less they have than the rich. Columnist David Brooks recounts a visit with a truck driver at a Carline County, Virginia, diner who "believed in the American Dream [and believed that] . . . he had achieved it." After all, the trucker could boast of all he owned. "He owned his own truck. He owned a nice house in Texas on a lake near the Louisiana border. His brother owned five trucks."[32]

Absolute standards of living certainly matter. But even here the story is not so simple. In the macho, fiercely independent world of long-haul trucking, for instance, it has gotten harder to own property. Truckers' pay has dropped dramatically since deregulation and with volatile gas prices. Brooks's trucker now has to hit the road for most of the year to earn a living. One of the themes we discuss in this book involves Americans' concerns about the struggle to make ends meet and to experience the American Dream in an age of rising economic inequality.

Despite these disputes over interpretation, there is now remarkably wide agreement that the distribution of income and wealth has shifted upward, even among those who were initially reluctant to accept the fact. President George W. Bush traveled to Wall Street in January 2007 to acknowledge that "income inequality is real [and has] been rising for more than twenty-five years."[33]

The sober chairman of the banker-oriented Federal Reserve Board, Ben Bernanke, has more fulsomely stated that economic inequality has risen, that it is a problem to be addressed, and that it can no longer be credibly denied. He devoted a recent speech to documenting that "inequality in economic outcomes has increased over time" and to outlining what to do about it.[34]

A *New York Times* series compiled recent data and interviewed some of the richest Americans to chronicle "[the recent] concentrated wealth [that] has made the early years of the 21st century truly another Gilded Age" comparable to the last Gilded Age before World War I.[35] Economic inequality has moved from chats in faculty lounges and academic conferences to headline news.

Where's the Class War?

Although the data on widening economic disparities are clear, some fear that doing something about it, or even talking about it, could ignite a class war. The original framers of the U.S. Constitution worried—as James Madison put it—about "the propensity of mankind to fall into mutual animosities." Writing in the wake of uprisings by small, struggling farmers, Madison warned that "the most common and durable source of factions has been the various and unequal distribution of property." "[T]he principal task of modern legislation," Madison held, was to "break and control the violence of faction"—namely, the "instability, injustice, and confusion" that consistently arises among "different classes."[36]

Open discussion of the unequal distribution of wealth and income tends to arouse Madison-type worries that the country may be teetering on the precipice of class war. Even raising the topic is sometimes derided as demagogic, pitting have-nots against the rich.

Columnist George Will sees America divided into warring camps: "liberalism's interest in diminishing inequality (using government power to regulate the economy's distribution effects) duels with conservatism's emphasis on freedom (incentives by which market forces rationally allocate wealth and opportunity)."[37] His concern is liberalism's unrelenting and uncompromising campaign on behalf of an "entitlement culture [that] subverts social peace by the proliferation of rival dependencies." The danger, Will warns, is that liberalism will "exacerbat[e] social conflicts—between generations . . ., between racial and ethnic groups . . ., and between all organized interests."[38] In other words, the problem facing America is that troublemakers are paying too much attention to economic inequality—which ordinary Americans would otherwise be indifferent to. This supposedly unwanted crusade is said to threaten America's sense of community.

Our analysis corroborates the fact that majorities of Americans do share a broad conservative inclination to safeguard individual liberty and to restrict government. But it also uncovers extensive evidence of *agreement,* not division, about dealing with inequality. Majorities of Americans of all economic and political stripes actually agree that economic inequality has widened, that this is worrisome, and that the government should respond. This wide agreement may seem particularly surprising in a time of historically sharp polarization between politicians and officials of the two political parties.

Even as the gulf between the rich and everyone else has widened, research on public opinion does not reveal an America breaking into hostile camps of the advantaged and the left-behind. Instead of class war, the evidence shows a high degree of positive, constructive agreement on what should be done. This book presents data from surveys conducted by us and by many other researchers that conclusively document Americans' broad agreement about inequality and its remedies.

The absence of pitched war between classes in the United States may seem remarkable in the face of America's widening economic gulfs and periodic alarms about envy among the less well-off. Three factors mentioned by political observers and scholars might be thought to account for the muting of class conflict and the supposed quiescence of lower-income people: lack of awareness of inequality; lack of concern about it; and opposition to government programs or taxes as remedies. But each of these explanations turns out to be off the mark. Let us look at each before we preview findings that refute them.

MUTED AWARENESS OR CONCERN ABOUT ECONOMIC INEQUALITY? Economic disparities might not seem particularly salient or alarming if Americans see them as generating incentives to work, excel, and take risks. Even advocates for reducing economic inequality like those on the editorial page of the *Washington Post* have cautioned that "[w]e do not claim that eliminating it is . . . desirable: Unequal rewards help motivate people to work and innovate."[39] Federal Reserve Chairman Bernanke agrees: "without the possibility of unequal outcomes tied to differences in effort and skill, the economic incentives for productive behavior would be eliminated, and our market-based economy—which encourages productive activity primarily through the promise of financial reward—would function far less effectively."[40]

The rich themselves are not shy about rationalizing their bursting bank accounts in such terms. Media and sports mogul Leo Hindery, Jr., makes the case that "there are people, including myself . . . who because of their uniqueness warrant whatever the market will bear." Citigroup founder Sanford Weill agrees, "the results that our company had . . . justified what I got." Insisting that the "income distribution has to stand" to motivate the entrepreneurs, Kenneth C. Griffin, chairman of the Citadel hedge fund, warns that "if the tax became too high, as a matter of principle I would not be working this hard."[41]

Ordinary Americans are said to share this tolerance for—or at least lack of alarm about—large economic gaps. We will see whether or not they do.

Americans might not particularly dislike economic inequality even if they are aware of it, for several possible reasons.

IS THE ECONOMIC REALM SPECIAL? In her important 1981 book *What's Fair?* Harvard professor Jennifer Hochschild presented a sophisticated account of why economic inequality would not be salient in the U.S. Americans, she argued, want and expect equality in politics, enshrined in the principle "one person, one vote." They want and expect equality in social relations. Aristocratic titles and bloodlines as well as race, ethnicity, gender, and other accidents of birth enjoy no legally recognized special status in America.

In the realm of the economy, however, Hochschild reported an acceptance of inequality. Based on some two dozen in-depth interviews in a midsized U.S. city, Hochschild insisted that Americans believe in material incentives and defer to individual self-reliance when it comes to private markets.[42]

Louis Hartz earlier situated such individualism in a deep historical and philosophical legacy. Hartz marveled that the individual liberty enshrined by the English philosopher John Locke "look[ed] like a sober description of fact [to Americans]. . . . [because their] society [was] sufficiently fluid to give a touch of meaning to the individualist norms of Locke."[43] In America, according to this meritocratic account, we are all born equal but then our talent and hard work separate us.

Permitting people to amass extreme riches, it is claimed, follows from a philosophical embrace of "freedom" and "liberty" that includes religious practice and the rights of speech and assembly, and extends to the whole realm of economic activity. We will see whether Americans actually embrace this view to the extent of being content with the current, high level of economic inequality.

DOES ECONOMIC STANDING DEFINE AMERICAN IDENTITIES? Americans, some observers assert, do not define themselves based on their income or wealth. Further describing his encounter with the truck driver at the Carline County, Virginia, diner, columnist David Brooks claimed the trucker had been "captured by the ethos" of trucking and country music. For "hard men" who embrace the "masculine mythology," Brooks is convinced that "social and moral categories generally trump economic ones." The result is that truckers identify with courageous "straight talkers" who struggle against adversity. They direct "their protests . . . not against the rich, but against the word manipulators—the lawyers, consultants, and the news media."[44]

The power of nonclass identities in America has impressed a long line of observers. Many historians, sociologists, and political scientists insist that Americans who share similar economic interests in the workplace have split into contending groups based on their ethnic and racial identities in their communities.[45]

OPPOSITION TO GOVERNMENT REMEDIES? Even if Americans were worried about economic inequality, they might not favor remedies involving government action. Governmental programs, it is claimed, are opposed because they curtail freedoms and opportunities, are costly, and only end up fuelling more government waste and inefficiency.

Columnist George Will attacks the "[s]teadily enlarging dependence on government" and, specifically, proposals for "a larger scope for interventionist government to circumscribe the market's role in allocating wealth and opportunity." Will salutes "conservativism's argument that excessively benevolent government is not a benefactor, and that capitalism does not merely make people better-off, it makes them better." The "essential" payoff of restrained government in deference to private markets is to encourage "a future orientation, self-reliance, [and] individual responsibility for healthy living." "[T]he dignity of individuals is bound up with the exercise of self-reliance and personal responsibility in pursuing one's interests."[46] For Will, this sort of conservatism enjoys popular support; the issue is whether politicians (even Republican politicians) remain faithful to it.

Will's well-articulated and principled conservatism could parallel more mundane concerns by Americans about any government action that might address economic inequality. Surveys have long shown that many Americans suspect widespread government waste, inefficiency, and corruption, and worry that government expansion will limit freedom. For instance, Bill Clinton's proposal to reform the health-care system was turned back by opponents who used warnings about threats to personal choice of medical care to build strong public resistance.

EDUCATIONAL EXCEPTIONALISM. As inequality has soared, pundits and politicians of both parties have latched onto rhetoric about government aid to education as a happy way to increase opportunities to escape economic stagnation while sustaining America's much-touted liberties and chances to get ahead. Many start with the proposition that "the reality [is] that the market increasingly rewards education and hard work."[47]

President Bush declared in his 2007 State of the Economy report that "[t]he reason [for income inequality] is clear: We have an economy that increasingly rewards education and skills." The source of income inequality, Bush argued, was that since "the 1970s, the market turned ferociously against the less skilled and the less educated." The remedy, Bush explained, is "[improving] skills and the government's job is to make sure we have an education system that delivers them." Bush heralded the No Child Left Behind law as "one of the most important economic initiatives of my presidency" because it "spend[s] federal money [and] expect[s] you at the local level to deliver results [that expand skills and thereby opportunity]."[48]

Many Democratic politicians agree, while complaining that President Bush and other Republican officials did not provide enough money to do the job.

Federal Reserve Chairman Bernanke similarly focuses on inadequate education as the "single greatest source of the long-term increase in inequality," and sees new education policy as the primary response to inequality because it makes "economic opportunity . . . as widely distributed and equal as possible." "[T]he challenge for policy is not to eliminate inequality per se but rather to spread economic opportunity as widely as possible" and to increase "national investment in education and training [in order to] reduce inequality while expanding economic opportunity." But Bernanke sets aside consideration of "tax and transfer policies that affect the distribution of income," as involving "difficult value judgments" that are "beyond the realm of objective economic analysis."[49]

Despite econometric studies showing a higher "rate of return" to education (college graduates now do far better than high-school-only workers do), there is in fact some doubt about whether much of the increase in economic inequality has actually resulted from educational disparities alone. There is notable inequality among college graduates themselves, and wage inequality has increased sharply at the same time that education levels have risen. American workers may have suffered more from a loss of economic and political power than from a "skills deficit."[50] Still, though educational policy is unlikely to be a panacea, there is little doubt that more equal educational opportunities would significantly reduce wage inequality in the United States. Later chapters will examine public thinking about educational and other policy remedies for inequality.

AVERSION TO TAXES? Even if Americans were concerned about inequality and were open to government responses, many observers accept as settled fact that the public will not pay for such programs with tax dollars. Americans are said to be extremely tax averse, unwilling to pay for public programs—even very appealing ones. If this is true, it is hard to escape the conclusion that government can do little about inequality because citizens are not willing to pay the bill.

The conundrum of how to pay for government remedies has haunted Washington for many years. The *Washington Post* editorial page wondered out loud: "Members of Congress appear to believe that calling for a tax increase—any tax increase—is political suicide. But can it really be true that voters are wedded to all of the tax cuts enacted this decade, even though the richest 1 percent stand to pocket more than a third of the windfall?"[51] This is yet another critical question that we will answer with extensive survey data.

Rejecting Myths and Rediscovering America

The three types of alleged public opposition to reducing inequality turn out to be largely myths. Like many myths they contain trace elements of truth, but they are fundamentally mistaken about what Americans actually think. We will see through these myths as we examine evidence from half a century of public-opinion surveys, together with our own uniquely detailed new survey. As fables give way to concrete evidence, we will rediscover an America that is indeed uneasy with government, but is pragmatic enough to swallow its reservations and offer strong and sustained support for concrete policies that would expand opportunity and reduce economic inequality.

PUBLIC ALARM OVER INEQUALITY. Claims that Americans are not aware of or concerned about economic inequality are incorrect. Large majorities of Americans from both major political parties and from across the income spectrum are alarmed about the high and increasing levels of inequality and want less inequality of incomes and wealth. Chapter 2 will show that ordinary Americans make generally accurate (if sometimes underestimated) assessments of inequalities in wealth and income. And they do not like what they see. About three-quarters of all Americans, including majorities of Republicans and the affluent, believe that the differences in income in America are too large. They recoil at today's Gilded Age.

Data on the real views of Americans have percolated up to some elites. Even as Federal Reserve Chairman Bernanke defends the benefit of economic inequality in motivating effort and rewarding skill, he also warns that "no one should be allowed to slip too far down the economic ladder, especially for reasons beyond his or her control." Why is America's top banker concerned? Negative public reaction. As inequality balloons, "the public at large might become less willing to accept the dynamism that is so essential to economic progress."[52] The *Washington Post*'s editorial page similarly worries that rising economic inequality "is bad for the social fabric."[53]

But Americans' concerns are not a distant possibility; they are a reality right now. Thus the labor-union movement has shifted its strategy toward campaigns that capitalize on the public's embrace of "minimum standards of decency that let people live a normal life," as S.E.I.U. union organizer Stephen Lerner explains. These standards feed into a highly visible "moral crusade" to force business heads and the affluent to "see the invisible workers as human beings, with bills to pay and kids to educate."[54]

The public's alarm over extreme and rising inequality does not mean that Americans are full-throated advocates for leveling economic differences, however. Nearly six out of ten Americans believe that wide income inequalities are probably necessary to motivate hard work. The public may even tilt toward greater acceptance of inequality than is recommended by some of America's rich and their bankers. Revered former Federal Reserve chairman Paul Volcker has challenged the claims of the very rich that their rewards have led them to create economic growth: "I don't see a relationship between the extremes of income now and the performance of the economy."[55]

Warren Buffet—who enjoys a fortune worth $46 billion from his investments and business acquisitions—concedes that he was "wired for asset allocation." He traces his success to his good fortune to be born in America, white, and male with a knack for spotting good economic bets.[56]

James Sinegal—chief executive of discount retailer Costco—believes that motivation can be generated with far lower levels of payoffs. Business heads, he predicts, would exert their "unique skills" for "$10 million instead of $200 million, if that were the standard."[57] Indeed, one Silicon Valley engineer concedes that "a lot of the money here is accidental money" that his neighbors receive without "setting out to become gazillionaires."[58]

Although there is wide agreement that some inequality motivates effort and resourcefulness, there is also significant disagreement about how much inequality is necessary. Prominent business leaders and policy makers are among those who doubt that hundreds of millions of dollars in salaries and stock options are necessary to generate strong work incentives. Indeed, comparisons with our economic competitors in Europe and elsewhere indicate that lower levels of inequality can generate comparable or even higher levels of productivity and economic growth.[59]

Protecting the American Dream
amidst Rising Economic Inequality

Close students of public opinion have known for at least forty years that the American public combines philosophical conservatism regarding the government's general role, with an equally strong pragmatic liberalism concerning concrete challenges facing Americans and specific government programs to help them.[60] It is important to resist the too common practice of forcing public opinion into rigid "liberal" or "conservative" categories.

The following chapters present abundant evidence about the complex attitudes of Americans. We note—and will offer fresh evidence on—Americans' conservative principles and instincts. But we will also document in detail the strong and sometimes overwhelming public support for specific government programs that would markedly decrease inequality.

Americans are simultaneously suspicious of government in the abstract and supportive of concrete government help in the face of real-world challenges. They turn to government to maintain or expand opportunities for individuals to pursue the American Dream and to provide minimal economic security for those who are left behind.

Posing philosophical conservatism and operational liberalism as polar opposites—a habit of both Right and Left—profoundly misunderstands Americans. The truth is that Americans seek concrete and targeted government programs in order to live the American Dream. They seek to protect opportunity in the face of rising economic inequality.

SUPPORT FOR CONCRETE GOVERNMENT REMEDIES. Political leaders of both parties are correct in judging that the public strongly supports educational initiatives to expand opportunity and create a society based on meritocracy in which work and education pay off. As we will see in chapter 3, this includes overwhelming support for expanded aid for preschool, elementary, and college education, and for retraining displaced workers.

What is particularly striking (and contrary to a great deal of conventional wisdom), however, is that—in order to provide both genuine opportunity and a measure of economic security—large majorities of Americans favor a number of specific government programs that go well beyond education policy. Chapter 3 also presents evidence of strong public support for government assistance to make sure that people can find jobs, get decent wages, have health-care coverage, be guaranteed adequate retirement pensions, and receive at least a minimal level of support if they cannot work. These programs would substantially reduce economic inequality in the United States.

Anxiety that addressing economic inequality might threaten social peace is misplaced. Support for these government programs comes from all sectors of society: from Republicans, from self-described middle-class and upper-class people, from whites, and from those with high incomes, as well as from Democrats, working-class people, African Americans, and lower-income citizens.

In reality, America largely agrees that action is needed. Will our elected officials listen?

AMERICANS ARE WILLING TO PAY TAXES. The charge that Americans are totally hostile to taxes has sometimes put a choke hold on policy debates. But it, too, is at odds with the evidence. The reality is that most Americans *are* in fact willing to pay taxes to fund concrete pragmatic programs to establish and protect individual opportunity.

Of course Americans don't enjoy paying taxes. For years, large majorities have called their own taxes too high. But this is only part of the story. Chapter 4 documents majority support among Americans (including majorities of Republicans and of the affluent) for using their tax dollars—and even paying higher taxes—to help fund concrete government programs targeted to jobs and wages, educational opportunity, and protections against illness or deprivation that rob Americans of the chance to make their way in the world. Contrary to noisy anti-tax rhetoric, the data show that fewer than one-third of Americans actually favor decreasing taxes in general, and only about one out of eight Americans want to cut estate taxes to zero on fabulously rich holdings. Majorities favor taxing the rich, and taxing them at higher rates than the less affluent.

A COUNTRY OF CONSERVATIVE EGALITARIANS. The reigning myth is that Americans don't care about economic inequality, hate government, intensely oppose taxes, and defer to the workings of private markets even if they strip individuals of opportunity and deprive them of the conditions to work their way up. This is not true.

Yes, Americans oppose "big government" and have reservations about taxes in the abstract. They are conservative philosophically. But Americans are pragmatists when private-market outcomes erode opportunity for themselves and their neighbors. Most Americans strongly and consistently support concrete government programs that protect genuine opportunity against the threat of widening economic inequality. Most support the taxes to pay for them. Put simply, Americans are conservative egalitarians, turning to government to sustain the conditions for individual opportunity.

These are not the slogans of "class war." Far from it. Americans agree across economic classes and political party loyalties.

The big question is whether our elected officials will respond. We take up that challenge in the conclusion.

2

Caring about Economic Inequality

The idea that Americans are aware of economic inequality and are quite concerned about it flies in the face of conventional views of America. To some, the very suggestion that Americans care about inequality borders on fantasy or, worse, invites dangerous demagogic appeals.

Despite such denials and warnings, solid evidence from surveys unmistakably demonstrates the truth: Americans know about, and worry about, the large and widening gap between the rich and everyone else. Far from engaging in a much-feared "class war," majorities of Americans from different political parties, different social classes, and different income groups *agree* that inequality exists, is a problem, and needs to be reduced.

A Word about Our Evidence

Before discussing how Americans think about inequality, we need to mention our sources of evidence about public attitudes. One source is an original national survey (the Inequality Survey) that was conducted for us during the summer of 2007.[1] A second source is an exhaustive search of past polls and surveys related to economic inequality since the 1930s.

We used past research to shape our own survey—to identify old questions that should be repeated, and to pinpoint new topics that should be examined afresh. As a result, our survey is not just a one-shot exercise to measure public opinion at one moment in time, but rather it brings up to date long-standing trends that stretch back in some cases to the 1930s. We are able both to study today's public attitudes and to see how they have changed over time. This is an enormous advantage. It greatly expands the amount of evidence at our disposal and allows us to confirm, update, or (in some cases) refute the main conclusions of previous researchers. (Most of the details about past findings are relegated to endnotes gathered at the end of the book; only major continuities or changes are mentioned in the text.)

In short, our rich and extensive body of survey data positions us to confirm and update patterns that are broadly accepted by all serious students of American public opinion, and also to present some new and startling findings.

We now turn to some reasons why Americans might not consider inequality much of a problem.

Why Americans Might Not Care Much about Inequality

Study after reputable study has shown economic inequality to be greater in the United States today than in the past, and greater than in European countries—all of which have vibrant private market economies. Yet there are reasons to expect that Americans might not care (or at least not care intensely) about our lopsided distributions of income and wealth.

"WORSHIP THE RICH—IT COULD BE ME." Human nature and American culture tend to exalt the rich. Sure, we sometimes resent the shallowness of movie stars or big-name business executives—

why would anyone spend hundreds of thousands of dollars on a champagne fountain? But periodic digs at the pettiness and bad behavior of a few super rich are accompanied by a deeper fascination with wealth and adulation of it.

Adam Smith—the often misunderstood icon of free-market advocates—recognized but strongly disapproved of the adulation of the rich. In a book devoted to good morality, he worried that the "disposition to admire, and almost to worship, the rich and the powerful, and to despise, or, at least, to neglect persons of poor and mean condition is the great and most universal cause of the corruption of our moral sentiments."[2]

In modern times, Smith's disdain for worship of the rich has given way to uninhibited adulation. Hollywood has ridden the fascination to the top of the rating charts. *The O.C.* shows off the travails of affluent teenagers in California's Orange County. *Laguna Beach* does much the same, while *The Hills* moves into the fashion world. Paparazzi favorite Donald Trump hosts a competition to select his next high-paid business assistant. (Is $250,000 a year enough to take Trump's abuse?)

The allure of the rich is partly voyeuristic. We enjoy a peek over the tall walls into home theaters, riding stables, and Italian-marbled, supersized bathrooms. But it is also based on hope. Glimpses of rich lifestyles offer a sort of "preview of coming attractions," a trailer about what any ambitious American might achieve if he or she works hard and sacrifices enough.

Washington Post and *Newsweek* columnist Robert J. Samuelson doubts that the public cares how rich Bill Gates is. "On the whole," Samuelson reasons, "Americans care less about inequality—the precise gap between the rich and the poor—than about opportunity and achievement."[3]

For many Americans, public displays of wealth are a reminder of our greatest myths—the rags-to-riches stories of Horatio Alger and Ben Franklin. (By the way, neither story is true—Alger was a second-generation Harvard man, and Franklin's story was puffed up after his death.)[4]

Americans don't care about inequality, according to one powerful account, because they want to be rich themselves. The American Dream is to move up to the mansion through hard work and tenacity. Political scientists Samuel Popkin and Henry Kim report that "most Americans do not equate inequality with injustice and will not sacrifice their own opportunities to help those who do not help themselves."[5]

While Hollywood portrays riches at the end of the rainbow, the news media spotlight our neighbors' work and sacrifice to realize the American Dream. Take Sharon Rhodes, who works for a Georgia manufacturer of custom mill work. With a middle-class background, divorced, and no college degree, she worked her way up to nearly a six-figure salary. She offers herself as the real face of American mobility—"If you are hard-working, if you apply yourself, I believe that you make your own luck."[6]

Ernie Frazier—a sixty-five-year-old Houston real-estate investor—agrees. Success, he explains, "has to do with a person's willingness to work hard." He is convinced that "the system is as fair as you can make it."[7]

Even when Americans wrestle with downsizing and layoffs, many remain optimistic about the benefits of working hard. Diana Lackey, a sixty-year-old homemaker and wife of a retired contractor in economically depressed upstate New York, remarked, "They call it the land of opportunity, and I don't think that's changed much."[8]

The chancellor of the New York City schools, Joel Klein, grew up in public housing and moved up the ladder. "I thought education would create opportunities my family didn't have. My father said if you want to grow up and not live in public housing, pay attention in school."[9]

Some of our political leaders—from members of Congress to presidents—themselves showcase the American Dream. Bill Clinton was born into a struggling family and moved up through education and hard work. So did Barack Obama.

Forbes magazine compiles lists of the four hundred wealthiest Americans. According to a recent list, only thirty-seven were given or inherited their wealth, compared to nearly half of those on the list two decades ago.[10] The "working rich" appear to be on the rise.

These success stories feature remarkable people. Although statistical research indicates that a *smaller* proportion of Americans are now able to move up the economic ladder (more on that later), the American Dream seems to provide a powerful rationale for inequality. Higher rewards for those who work harder and are smarter are said to generate incentives for a vibrant and expanding economy that could benefit everyone.

Larry Kudlow, host of CNBC's *Kudlow & Co.* and an editor at the *National Review*, praises inequality and the drive to work hard to succeed and become rich. "I'm not denying that there's inequality," Kudlow says. Far from it. "[T]here should be inequality, that's what capitalism is all about." Reading from the prayer book of the American creed, Kudlow preaches: "The free-market system has equality of opportunity," which opens the door for the hard working and lubricates a prosperous economy that benefits everyone else.[11]

Another set of commentators object to how inequality is publicly portrayed. "[D]iscussions of income distribution," one group reports, are "inherently misleading. . . . [because] income is not distributed, it is earned." They protest that higher-income Americans are vilified as "at best lucky and at worst criminal" when "differences in income relate directly to differences in work." The reality, they insist, is that "[f]or the most part, upper-income American families do better than lower-income families because they work more" while those in the lower end of the income spectrum rarely work as hard or at all. They "question whether the fact that harder work is typically rewarded with higher incomes really constitutes 'inequality.'"[12]

We socialize young children to work hard and pay attention in school, and we hope that these efforts produce broadly shared economic and social benefits for our communities. As one economist explains, "Most people are working very hard to transmit their advantages to their children. And, that's quite a good thing."[13]

Most Americans do indeed have deep faith in the American Dream and in the rewarding of hard work and skill. But we should not automatically assume that this tranquilizes the public against caring about inequality. As we show below, Americans *both* embrace the

American Dream and recoil from the extreme, growing gap between the rich and everyone else. In fact it appears that the hope and expectation of living the American Dream is actually leading majorities of Americans of diverse backgrounds to *oppose* extreme inequality, as unfairly curtailing opportunity to all and stacking the deck in favor of the rich and their offspring.

FINDING WALDO—WE ALL LOOK THE SAME. Imagine a world without Paris Hilton, Donald Trump, or racks of magazines that beam out images of the wealthy's Land of Oz. Would we notice the rich?

A century ago, everyday life was filled with markers of wealth, from clothing, speech, and entertainment to religious affiliation and home address. Those with money were white, attended the stiff-backed Protestant churches (often Episcopalian), and were educated at Ivy League colleges. "They" stood out, by design.

Workplace environments were elaborately choreographed with clear norms and rules of hierarchy. Factory workers and clerks were openly treated as unequal to owners and managers. Each had their "place." Bosses were addressed by formal title or as "Mr." (rarely "Miss" or "Mrs."), a hit-or-miss occurrence today. Administrative staff were "secretaries," by whom curt orders were expected to be fulfilled without question. Underlings were expected to follow etiquette in style and comportment.

The least well-off stood out by what they lacked or by deliberate efforts to stigmatize them. The English at one point used a red-hot brand to literally scar the flesh of poor people who depended on government aid for survival.

Today, everyday markers of wealth and poverty exist, of course, but they are blurred. Low-wage factories around the world flood America with inexpensive consumer goods, from shoes and dresses to cell phones and electronic gadgets. What used to be high-end fashion is now outnumbered by discount imitations. Torn or beaten-up clothes may be considered fashionable, not markers of deprivation. High-end sports cars have their Ford or Chrysler knockoffs.

Barriers of race, religion, and educational background seem to have receded. Blacks, Jews, Catholics, and Mormons can all be found leading businesses and government. The bosses less often come from an "Ivy" school.

In American workplaces, stores, and neighborhoods, workers and bosses are often outwardly treated as coequal colleagues or acquaintances. Formal distinctions have faded. CEO Smith may be called "Joe." It is the height of poor manners today for a manager to brusquely order around a staff member. Better to ask a question in a low-key manner and welcome feedback from a "team" member.

This leveling of social distinctions in our ordinary interactions tends to create an appearance of "sameness" in everyday life. The affluent no longer automatically stand out.

The absence of everyday symbols of stark social distinctions may fuel a sense of contentment for what Americans have, reducing awareness of what they lack or others have more of. Wanda Brown—fifty-eight-year-old wife of a retired planner for the Puget Sound Naval Shipyard—enjoys the pride of having grown up poor and now being able to declare "we are comfortable and we are middle class and our son is better off than we are."[14]

Statistical evidence of large and widening economic disparities may now be easier to ignore: "out of sight, out of mind." Americans may literally not see the divides and may instead focus on the slice of society's pie that they do get.

AMERICAN CONSERVATISM. Americans might recognize the wide and growing disparity of income and wealth and yet remain unalarmed, owing to their genuinely conservative philosophical orientation, and specifically their disposition to favor hard work and material rewards.

Two themes resonate in Americans' economic conservatism. First, most Americans accept a substantial degree of inequality. They do not want to "level" all incomes. They oppose putting limits on how much people can earn and they do not envy or resent the rich.[15]

Public-opinion experts Everett Carll Ladd and Karlyn Bowman found that Americans accept and even welcome the affluent. Sixty-two percent of the public conclude that America "benefit(s) from having a class of rich people." Only a fifth of Americans agree that the rich "keep the common man from his proper share of the wealth," and only 29 percent attribute "many of society's ills" to the rich. Even when pressed about millionaires, majorities or solid pluralities report that society would be worse off without them.[16]

Our own Inequality Survey confirms that Americans recognize the merits of allowing some degree of economic inequality. They firmly reject the idea everyone should be paid the same amount. When we asked how much people in different occupations should be paid, we were consistently told that CEOs, heart surgeons, doctors in general practice, and owners of small shops (in that order) should earn substantially more than skilled factory workers, and much more than unskilled factory workers or sales clerks.

A second theme in Americans' economic conservatism is that they believe inequality drives work and accomplishment. Fifty-eight percent of those we interviewed told us that, in order to get people to work hard, large differences in pay are "probably" or "absolutely" necessary (most said "probably.")[17] (While a majority of Americans recognize the likely motivational power of inequality for individuals, however, we will see below that most actually doubt that large differences in pay are necessary to fuel prosperity for the society as a whole.)

The public's conservatism is widely embraced; it is not limited to a small segment of the population. Research by Stanley Feldman and John Zaller reveals that even self-identified liberals harbor unease toward government and potential infringements on individuals.[18] In our own survey, solid majorities of Democrats[19] (58 percent) and of low-income earners[20] (62 percent) said that large differences in pay are probably necessary to get people to work hard (see fig. 2.1).

Americans fundamentally accept the fact that private markets allocate more income and wealth to some than to others. They reject radical redistribution that would level the differences. The authen-

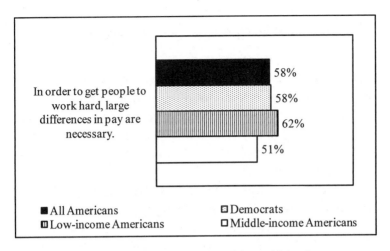

In order to get people to work hard, large differences in pay are necessary.

58%
58%
62%
51%

■ All Americans
▥ Low-income Americans
▣ Democrats
▢ Middle-income Americans

FIGURE 2.1 Americans, including Democrats and those with low incomes, accept some inequality. Source: Inequality Survey.

tic conservatism of ordinary Americans tells only one side of our country's story, however. Alongside conservatism stands a strong tendency toward pragmatism and a belief that everyone should enjoy genuinely equal opportunity. Americans' pragmatism sits uneasily with their conservative inclinations and, at times, overtakes them.

LIVING IN THE REAL WORLD. Americans live in the present, alert to the concrete challenges and threats they and their neighbors face. They may dream the American Dream, but they live day to day with eyes wide open. Indeed, the high expectations of Americans—that everyone should have the opportunity to translate hard work into generous rewards—make them acutely attentive to barriers that unfairly advantage others and deny them their own chance. Far from being unaware or uninterested in inequality, Americans are sensitive to lost opportunities and to the unfairness of undeserved riches going to a few. They demand a society that is truly modeled on the American Dream.

These concerns lead to a keen and reasonably accurate awareness of high and rising inequality in income and in wealth.

Eyes Wide Open—Inequality of Incomes

The reality is that Americans have long recognized economic disparities. Three decades of surveys have regularly shown that about seven or eight out of ten Americans believe that "the rich get richer and the poor get poorer." Leslie McCall, analyzing these and other survey questions, concludes that "despite the prevailing image that Americans are tolerant of inequality, well over half of the population thinks that inequality is too high."[21]

Our Inequality Survey confirms these earlier findings. Although Americans accept the idea that unequal pay motivates hard work, a solid majority (59 percent) *disagree* with the proposition that large differences in income are "necessary for America's prosperity."

Our survey probed further into Americans' awareness and understanding of discrepancies between the incomes earned by people who work in different occupations.

We asked those we interviewed to estimate the annual dollar amounts (before taxes) taken home by people in a variety of jobs—from general-practice doctor, heart surgeon, and boss of a large national corporation to department-store sales clerk, small-shop owner, and unskilled or skilled worker in a factory.[22] These were "open-ended" questions, asking for actual dollar amounts rather than merely a choice from a fixed list of options. Few had any trouble coming up with responses.[23]

The responses told us several striking things. One is that Americans think about how much others earn. All but a few readily made estimates of annual incomes. And these estimates were not wild-eyed flights of the imagination; they had solid connections with reality.

SEEING DIFFERENCES. Americans perceive very large differences in the wages and salaries accruing to different occupations. Doctors and corporate executives are seen as earning a lot more than ordinary workers. The annual earnings of general-practice doctors were estimated as $130,000, heart surgeons were pegged at $250,000, and corporate heads were put at $500,000. (These estimates are median or midpoint figures. That is, they are figures that landed in the middle of the approximations offered by those we interviewed.)[24] The estimated salaries of the doctors and corporate titans were far higher than what Americans believe sales clerks and skilled or unskilled workers bring home each year—from six times higher to more than eleven times higher. As we will see, most Americans think this is too much inequality.

The sensitivity of Americans to differences in incomes is not merely idle guesswork or a passing fancy. It is the kindling that ignites disputes and high-profile controversies that land in community newspapers.

Madison, Wisconsin, was the site of a nasty fight between teachers and school board president Juan Lopez, whom the teachers had helped sweep into office but who then voted against their contract and set off a strike. One teacher walking the picket line—Pat DiBiasse—bitterly complained of reports that "Juan said teachers make too much money." "The problem," according to DiBiasse, "is not that teachers make too much money." "Some doctors make too much money. Professional athletes make too much money. Corporate CEOs make too much money." But for DiBiasse and others on the picket line, "Nurses, social workers, fast-food workers, secretaries and a lot of other people make too little money."[25]

Although the culture of sameness may have removed many nineteenth-century social distinctions, the real-world struggle of middle-income earners sometimes puts into sharp relief the life of the rich.

San Jose, California, offers especially sharp contrasts. Construction crews at the airport are building a hangar for another fleet of private jets owned by Silicon Valley's better-off. Meanwhile, the middle class struggles to pay for housing, health-care costs, and other essentials. Take train conductor Terrence Dicks, who works the line through San Jose. Dicks earns $63,000 a year and finds it difficult to be a "regular Joe." "People in the middle," he explains, "they are definitely pinched."[26]

And, if Dicks thinks too hard about what he lacks and not what he has, he is readily reminded that his job is one that many Americans would like. Even before the economic crash, some 10 to 12 percent of Americans regularly said that they were very likely or fairly likely to lose their jobs in the next year.[27] Many more are anxious about their future and about the prospects for their friends and neighbors.

Scott Clark would have job envy. He lost his well-paid job building submarines. Scott picked up a delivery-service job that pays far less and forces him to work from 2 a.m. to about 3 in the afternoon. Job conditions? He drives in the middle of the highways around Richmond, Virginia, to "give me a chance if a deer runs in from either direction." Gone are OSHA protections, let alone health and pension coverage and plans for retirement by his midfifties.[28]

According to the catechism of the American Dream, working hard and getting a good education is the secret to success. But college-age kids are discovering a little secret. Winning the lottery of admission to a good college does not neatly follow the Horatio Alger myth about getting ahead on your own merit. It turns out that getting into the elite colleges may require a veritable consulting team of advisers, test coaches, application gurus, and, for some, ghostwriting essayists. Guess who can afford the consultants and experts (let alone the tuition money). It usually is not folks from middle- or lower-income families.

Take the case of Kevin Robinson, in eastern Pennsylvania. His single mom, who works in a state transportation office, lacked the money to pay for consultants or preparers. To Kevin, "I felt it was unfair that other applicants had tutoring and things like that." Kevin's mom cuts to the chase. "It frustrates me to know there isn't a level playing field. You have some kids with options and advantages that others don't. And the colleges have no way of knowing. They think they're comparing apples and apples when they're not."[29]

Down on the street, differences in income and what it means can become obvious. Inequality is not an abstract notion raised by outside troublemakers. Americans see inequality because they live it.

The advantages of the better-off are irritating to the middle class. They are enraging to Americans who are struggling to make ends meet.

M. D. Richberg earned a bachelors degree but lost his job of twenty-two years when the rehabilitation center in Dayton, Ohio, closed. He was hit with a pay cut of $12,000 to take another job. "It's been devastating," Richberg reports, "I'm barely holding on." "My son had to drop out of college.... [and] there's no upward mobility and no overtime."[30]

Donald Roberts—an unskilled worker in Dayton supporting a disabled wife and two children—struggles to pay his bills by working two jobs that pay a bit more than minimum wage. "I guess I could quit a job, keep the [Medicaid] insurance and not have a place to live or enough to pay my bills," he speculates before revealing his frustration—"They make it practically impossible these days for a person busting his butt trying to provide for his family."[31]

SEEING THE TRUTH. Americans rather accurately estimate the income of the kinds of people they know personally. Table 2.1 shows that they are close to the mark when sizing up how much sales clerks and factory workers take home each year. For unskilled factory workers, Americans estimated $22,000 when in fact (at the time of the survey) they earned between $16,000 and $20,000. Sales clerks were pegged at $22,000 and actually earned about $26,000. The estimates of GP doctors' earnings, too, came fairly close to reality, but the incomes of heart surgeons were seriously underestimated.[32]

Americans know that the rich take home a lot more. But as if estimating how far away Betelgeuse is, they can't fathom how much more. Corporate bosses were seen as pulling in half a million dollars per year—more than twenty times the estimates for unskilled workers and sales clerks. The reality is that, at the time of the survey, CEOs of S&P 500 companies reaped about $14,000,000 per year: seven hundred times more than the average factory worker and 540 times more than sales clerks.[33] Forbes.com in 2007 listed eight CEOs with total compensation of more than $100 million each. (Forbes, no enemy of business, noted little connection between pay and performance.)[34]

How would Americans react if they understood that the gap between what their neighbors earn and the jackpot lottery that corporate bosses win every year is nearly thirty times as great as they

TABLE 2.1 Americans know their neighbors' incomes, but underestimate those of the affluent

	Real-world annual income	Perceived annual income (median estimate)
Unskilled factory worker		$22,000
production worker	$16,000	
machine operator	$20,000	
Sales clerk	$26,000	$22,000
Skilled factory worker	$44,000	$40,000
Owner of a small shop	$60,000	$50,000
Doctor in general practice	$185,000	$130,000
Heart surgeon	Over $400,000	$250,000
CEO of a large national corporation	Over $14,000,000	$500,000

Sources: Real-world income, simplyhired.com, November 8, 2007, and January 9, 2008; indeed.com, November 8, 2007; 2007 AMGA survey at cejkasearch.com; HR survey by salary.com; Corporate Library survey reported at aflcio.org/corporatewatch/paywatch. Perceived annual income, Inequality Survey, 2007.

think? One can imagine that the existing opposition to inequality would be even greater.

Although the magnitude of the gap between the rich and average workers is unfathomable for most Americans, they clearly do appreciate that the gap is large and growing. A 2007 Pew survey found 63 percent of Americans saying that the country is "losing ground" on the gap between rich and poor.[35]

Eyes Wide Open—Wealth Inequality

The distribution of wealth appears to be less of a mystery to ordinary Americans. Most have a fairly good idea of what wealth is. It consists of your house's value (subtracting mortgage debt), your money in a bank, and any stock, bonds, or other assets you own. Income is what comes in from earnings, dividends, and so forth; wealth consists of material possessions or resources.

SEEING DIFFERENCES. Americans know that wealth in the U.S. is very highly concentrated. Part of this is obvious. You can see that Bill Gates lives in a mansion and that Donald Trump's cars—including a Cadillac DTS Executive Limo and a Mercedes-Benz SLR McLaren—are worth a fortune.[36]

Kevin Godsea, who works for the U.S. Fish and Wildlife Service in Fort Myers, Florida, concludes that "the wages of middle class workers are stagnant" but that the "ultra-rich and the rich continue to have mechanisms to make money like the stock market." This isn't the talk of a flaming liberal Democrat; Godsea is a registered Republican watching with uncertainty as his world changes.[37]

The Americans we interviewed offered an astounding estimate of how much wealth is held by a tiny number of people. The median response was that the richest 1 percent hold fully 50 percent of all the wealth in the country.[38] And an overwhelming 81 percent of Americans believe that the gap in wealth between wealthy Americans and middle-class Americans has gotten larger in the past twenty-five years.

The concentration of wealth among a few is not new. The rich have been around a long time. Some pundits and politicians are fond of insisting that "all boats are rising"—those owned by the rich and by the lower- and middle-income classes as well. The problem today, as one expert explains, is that "the rich [are] getting richer and nobody else [is] making much progress."[39]

It does not take a Ph.D. in economics to spot the obvious. Dana Eichelberger works at a shoe store in Hanover, Pennsylvania. Her life has taught her that "the rich are just going to keep on getting richer and the poor are going to keep on getting poorer."[40]

SEEING THE TRUTH. The Americans we interviewed were a bit high in their estimate of wealth inequality, but they came fairly close to the mark. Table 2.2 shows that our interviewees estimated that the super rich controlled half of the country's wealth, while in the real world 1 percent of U.S. households own about one-third (34.3 percent) of all the net wealth. This figure rises to 42.2 percent if we focus on net

TABLE 2.2 Americans size up the fabulous wealth of the rich

	Real-world: Wealth held by richest 1 percent	Perception: Median estimate of wealth held by richest 1 percent
Super rich (including home equity)	34.3% (2004)	50%
Super rich (excluding home equity)	42.2% (2004)	

Sources: Real-world, Edward N. Wolff, "Recent Trends in Household Wealth in the United States" (working paper 502, Levy Economics Institute of Bard College, June 2007), 11. Perception, Inequality Survey, 2007.

financial wealth, excluding home equity—which is the most widely held asset.[41] (Millions of Americans hold no positive net worth at all except in their homes. The dangers of treating home equity as a usable asset became painfully evident when home prices plunged.)

The public's perceptions of an increase in the wealth gap over the last twenty-five years may or may not be correct in terms of the precise timing, but the concentration of wealth has increased greatly since World War II and has probably increased since the 1960s. The top 1 percent of super rich households held 125 times more wealth than that of the median household in 1962 (impressive enough); by 2004, it controlled 190 times more. Put in dollar terms, the average net wealth of the super rich in the top 1 percent was nearly $15,000,000 in 2004 compared to about $83,000 for the bottom 80 percent.[42]

Americans Oppose Growing Inequality

Americans are awake to the stark and growing gap between the income and wealth of the super rich and everyone else. And they don't like it.

Nearly three quarters (72 percent) of Americans agree that "differences in income in America are too large."

Two-thirds (68 percent) reject the idea that the current distribution of money and wealth is "fair." Instead, this large majority says that "the money and wealth in this country should be more evenly distributed among a larger percentage of the people."

Jane Huntley, aged seventy-seven, a retired elementary school teacher in New York state, is alarmed that "we are creating have and have-not classes in this country."[43]

These are not just fleeting results from one survey. Americans' basic opposition to inequality has been evident since at least the mid-1980s. Figure 2.2 shows that about six out of ten Americans have consistently favored having money and wealth "more evenly distributed" and have rejected the proposition that it was already fairly distributed. This remarkable finding comes from eleven surveys conducted between 1984 and 2007. Our 2007 survey detected a twenty-year high point in support for a more even distribution of money and wealth.[44]

Let us look beyond broad generalizations about wealth and income to consider how Americans respond to differences in pay for specific

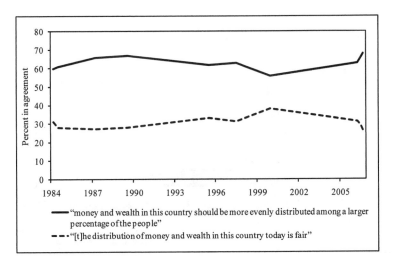

FIGURE 2.2 Americans favor more even distribution of money and wealth. Source: Gallup; *Los Angeles Times*, April 1985; Inequality Survey, June 2007.

occupations. After all, we would expect Americans' conservatism to lead them to support higher pay for CEOs and for doctors who save lives.

Americans do in fact want people in occupations that require more responsibility and skill to be paid more. Radical equalizers should take note—Americans do not believe that everyone should be paid the same amount.

But Americans do believe that the enormous economic gulfs in our country should be narrowed (not eliminated). This striking finding emerges from comparing how much the public believes that different occupations *actually* earn, with how much Americans say they *should* earn. For each of the occupations about which we had asked how much they "ACTUALLY earn," we also asked how much they "SHOULD earn."

In figure 2.3 we put answers to both types of question together. The figure reveals that the public favors two changes from the situation it perceives to exist now: more pay for lower-income occupations, and less pay for the highest-income occupations. Sales clerks and factory workers should earn $5,000 more a year (about 23 percent

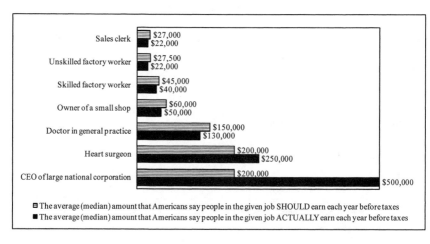

FIGURE 2.3 Americans favor paying low-wage workers more and CEOs less. Source: Inequality Survey.

more), according to the median responses of those we interviewed. Even general-practice doctors—already seen as doing pretty well—are slotted by Americans to receive more than what they are believed to be earning now.

By contrast, Americans favor reducing the pay of heart surgeons. And they want to cut the income of corporate titans by more than half—from the perceived $500,000 to a desired $200,000. Imagine the reaction of ordinary working Americans if they learned that the CEOs of major national corporations actually pull in $14 million a year.

No Class War

Economic inequality is often portrayed as dividing rich from poor and Republicans from Democrats. Since the New Deal of the 1930s, Republican and Democratic officials in Washington have often battled about whether and how to deal with economic inequality.

Politicians and pundits who don't much care about inequality frequently slam public discussion of it as demagoguery aimed at seeding division and discord, irresponsibility exposing uneasy fault lines just under the surface.

The truth confounds Madisonian warnings about the "violence of factions." It contrasts oddly with the political acrimony among some of today's Washington power brokers. The fact is that most Americans are already aware of the stark economic inequality in America, and most want to see it reduced.

And the majorities who favor reducing inequality are not scary mobs of landless seventeenth-century peasants with pitchforks.

Americans from widely different backgrounds agree that extreme inequality of income and wealth is bad and should be dealt with. This includes low-income groups struggling to make ends meet and Democrats committed to a philosophy of social justice. But supporters of reducing inequality also include most Republicans, most citizens who consider themselves "middle class,"[45] and most higher-income people.

Figure 2.4 shows that solid majorities of Republicans[46] (56 percent)

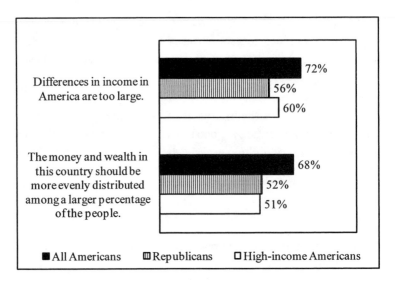

FIGURE 2.4 Americans, including Republicans and those with high incomes, want to reduce inequality. Source: Inequality Survey.

and of high income earners[47] (60 percent) agree that income differences are "too large" in the United States.

Remarkably, then, majorities of those who are often assumed to be *least* concerned about inequality believe that income differences in the United States are too large. They also favor doing something about it. Majorities of Republicans (52 percent) and of the affluent (51 percent) favor more evenly distributing money and wealth. Stop the presses! Most upper-income Americans and most rank-and-file Republicans favor redistribution to narrow the cavernous gaps between the rich and everyone else. Many well-off people go beyond narrow economic self-interest and care about what is happening to others.

A substantial number of government officials and politicians agree with these ordinary Americans in disapproving of today's inequality. They include Democrats like John Edwards and Barack Obama, but also prominent Republicans, and Federal Reserve chair Ben Bernanke. Bernanke has publicly insisted that policy makers "must try to ensure that the benefits of global economic integration are sufficiently widely shared."[48] Bush administration Treasury Secretary Paulson has similarly called attention to the reality that "many [Americans] aren't seeing significant increases in their take-home pay [because]. . . . [t]heir increases in wages are being eaten up by high energy prices and rising health care costs." Seeking to find common ground with other policy makers, he suggested that "[i]t is neither fair nor useful to blame any political party."[49]

Clearly, Americans are not engaged in a class war based on economic self-interest or partisan loyalties. Of course lower-income groups and Democrats tend to be more inclined to denounce income differences and to call for redistribution. But the most striking finding is the majoritarian agreement among Americans of different classes and parties—and racial groups as well.[50]

America, We Have a Problem

One of the great paradoxes of our time is that certain outward appearances of equality may be at a historic high point just as hard economic data demonstrate that *inequality* has hit its highest level since the Great Depression of the 1930s. Economic disparities are high and rising, but without the old outward signs. Out of sight, bread lines and soup kitchens are in fact facing high demand, but we are not seeing long lines like those captured by the iconic photographs from the Great Depression.

Make no mistake about it. Americans may appear outwardly equal, but inequality does exist. It is causing damage and sometimes anger.

Damage from inequality is all around us. We see it creep into policy debates. The vicious (and fanciful) proposals to wall off America from immigration and to deport the twelve million illegal immigrants already here reflect, in part, a lashing out at a perceived threat to low-paying jobs. The growing resistance to international trade is another sign of economic uncertainty. Immigration and trade policies may offer collective benefits to the country as a whole, but they have become resented symbols for millions of Americans who are worried about making ends meet or holding their spot at the economic table.

Two pillars of America's banks and businesses—Federal Reserve Chairman Bernanke and Treasury Secretary Paulson—call for reducing inequality in order to stem the erosion of public support for policies they see as critical to the country's interests, including openness to trade and immigration.

The damage from inequality extends beyond policy debates. It is sapping the moral foundation of our economic and social system— the notion of equal opportunity and the promise that rewards will flow to those who educate themselves and work hard. Attainment of the American Dream can still be found in the successes of certain remarkable Americans. But these are exceptions to a general pattern of dwindling opportunity.

A growing number of rigorous, independent studies demonstrate that the movement of Americans up the economic ladder has stagnated or declined. A prominent component of America's private-banking system—the Federal Reserve Bank of Boston—reported that fewer families have been able to climb the income ladder since the 1970s. A nonpartisan federal government agency, the Bureau of Labor Statistics, found that mobility actually decreased in the 1990s from where it had been in the 1980s.[51] Using rigorous statistical models scrutinized by independent experts, these studies reach similar conclusions based on very different approaches—from comparing the economic success of parents and their children and tracking the income of families over many years to tracing the incomes of brothers over time.

These findings may be new to researchers, but they are lived every day by millions of Americans who find the value of their paychecks stagnating or declining while their costs for food, energy, and health care are rapidly rising. A researcher in the country's heartland reports that "Middle America and Middle Iowans are getting squeezed."[52] An

Iowa union official who used to represent jobs that put workers in the middle class matter-of-factly reports, "I'm pretty convinced that I will be part of the last generation that will do better than my parents." The implication is obvious: "A lot of people in my age group agree the American dream is slowly fading away."[53]

In Virginia, Chuck Moore got the college degree and white-collar job, but he now finds himself at thirty-five without a job and unable to find work that even matches his starting salary. Concluding that he had no options, he signed up to work at an animal hospital. He's fallen from a professional white-collar occupation to cleaning out kennels, at half his previous salary with no benefits. Capturing the sense of "Dream withdrawn" that is shared by many Americans, Moore blurts out "there's something not right about that."[54] Scott Clark—the 2 a.m. delivery guy who drives in the middle of the road to avoid deer—reflects at the end of the day that he's struggled but still managed to cobble together middle-income pay. But whether his kids will be able to hold on is another matter: "It's just too uncertain. . . . There's nothing you can just count on. I wish there was."[55]

Affluent Americans and Republicans appear concerned about the uncertainty facing middle- and lower-income Americans. The support of GOP and higher-income majorities for diminishing inequality reveals an appreciation for the threats posed by inequality.

Shrinking opportunity and the fear of falling behind may contribute to widespread distrust of government and skepticism about the potential for improvement. Clark is a bipartisan politician hater. He greeted promises to rebuild the middle class from Democratic presidential wannabees with a derisive, "Yeah, right." He flat out nailed President George W. Bush as "a liar" for echoing that call.

Americans see inequality and they don't like it. The bonds that connect us as neighbors are threatened. Our public discussions of policy issues are harder to conduct and decisions harder to reach. A student of Pennsylvania's economic struggles distilled the widening impacts of inequality: "Our economic system depends on people's faith in it. . . . The rising inequality we're seeing has the potential of undermining that faith."[56] The casualties include the life dreams of Americans and their trust in our economic and political systems.

Contrary to conventional wisdom, then, most Americans are aware of the high and growing economic inequality in the United States. Most want to ameliorate the situation. But do they want the government to do it? Conventional wisdom says no. In the next chapter we will see that this conventional wisdom, too, is wrong. Large majorities of Americans favor many concrete, specific government policies that would reduce economic inequality.

3

Looking to
Government for Help

Americans turn out to be aware of and concerned about economic inequality. They are not ignorant, unconcerned, or acquiescent. But do they want the government to do anything about it?

Mention of "government" triggers associations with today's political Hatfield and McCoy rivalry—Democrat versus Republican. You can predict what most Republican and Democratic politicians will say in public about government. The well-worn script (you fill in the actors' names) has the Republican extolling the value of private markets and bemoaning the evils of government, while the Democrat evokes the plight of the downtrodden and calls for social justice, closing with a plea for a new government program and taxes to pay for it—which upon closer inspection may not quite cover the tab.

This movie is into multiple reruns, and it does describe part of what goes on in Washington. Republican strategist Grover Norquist bragged that "my goal is to cut government in half in twenty-five years to get it down to the size where we can drown it in the bathtub."[1] Congressmen Newt Gingrich, Dick Armey, and others put together the "Contract with America" to roll back government and taxes. On the other side, Democrats often do favor more government programs and higher taxes on the wealthy.

Here comes the big "but." The public fracas obscures important areas of agreement inside the halls of government. Many or most Democrats in Congress actually support markets, are skeptical about government, resist pressure from their supporters to hike spending as much as they'd like, and vote for tax cuts. Many or most Republicans vote for numerous government programs that run the gamut from national-defense initiatives to the new Medicare prescription-drug benefits to the No Child Left Behind law that radically thrust the federal government into state and local decisions about educating students from kindergarten through high school. Members of both parties support subsidies for businesses and programs for their constituents back home, whether farmers wanting price supports or suburbanites wanting new bike paths. The much-ballyhooed "Bridge to Nowhere," costing $200 million to connect the tiny Alaskan hamlet of Ketchikan with its airport on the equally obscure island of Gravina, was proposed in 2005 by one of the most senior Republicans in the U.S. Senate.

But what do ordinary Americans think about government? Some—especially devotees of the major political parties—may be conditioned like Pavlov's dogs to simply react by habit to the rhetoric of their tribal leaders. What's striking, however, is that most Americans are not so easily programmed. Surprisingly large majorities defy the stereotypes of "government haters" or "collectivizers." They want individuals to take care of themselves rather than relying on massive government handouts, yet at the same time they back concrete government programs to help individuals have genuine opportunities to pursue the American Dream. If government policies actually followed this combination of principled conservatism and pragmatic liberalism, they would have the effect of decreasing (though not completely closing) the gaps that have been widening between middle-income Americans and the super rich.

Overwhelming evidence of Americans' support for pragmatic

government action has not prevented a lot of fuss, well intentioned or not, that would obscure or deny the public's conservative egalitarianism in the face of concrete threats to the American Dream.

Philosophical Conservatism about Government

The America presented to us by some pundits and politicians is like a cartoon caricature. Some features are familiar, but the overall effect is hardly recognizable. A familiar part is Americans' philosophical conservatism.

DREAMS OF BECOMING RICH. In the abstract, Americans think there is already a great deal of economic opportunity for individuals, and they tend to distrust government. Figure 3.1 shows that three-quarters of all Americans, including very large majorities of Democrats and low-income earners, believe it is "still possible" to start out poor in this country, work hard, and become rich. Belief in the American Dream cuts across lines of class and race. Large majorities of whites, nonwhites, and low-income whites, and even a majority of *unskilled* white workers agree that it is possible to start out poor and become rich.[2]

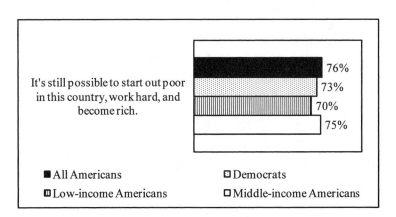

FIGURE 3.1 Americans, including Democrats and the less affluent, embrace the American Dream. Source: Inequality Survey.

Belief in the possibility of the American Dream is widespread and durable, but it should not be exaggerated. "Possible" does not mean probable, and (as noted in earlier chapters) real-world upward mobility is rather limited. One estimate holds that a child born into the bottom tenth of income earners actually has less than a 2 percent chance of making it into the top tenth.[3] Nonetheless, the fact remains—documented by polls since 1983—that majorities of Americans doggedly believe in the rags-to-riches story.[4]

President George W. Bush's campaign for partially privatizing Social Security (allowing individuals to invest part of their payroll contributions in the stock market) attempted to tap into America's attraction to hitting the jackpot. Gus Piliafas, who works for General Motors and lives near Flint, Michigan, supported the president's proposal because "It gives people the option to invest in the private sector. . . . [and once enacted] I think that I'd be a millionaire." He acknowledged that "It's a gamble, but it's a gamble worth taking."[5]

Belief in opportunity and in the potential to strike it rich buttresses public support for the private-enterprise system. Figure 3.2 shows that large majorities of Americans, including majorities of Democrats and low-income earners, agree that "our freedom depends on the free enterprise system" and that the government "must always protect private property." (Again, majority support cuts across lines of race as well as class and party.)[6] In endorsing protection of private property, respondents rejected the alternative that "the government can sometimes take private property" (without mention of full compensation) when it "needs to do something badly enough," for example, build an interstate highway or a post office.[7]

Even in the face of sharply higher economic inequality, many policy makers return to this bedrock trust that individuals can seize opportunity in the private sector. President George W. Bush argued that "the question is whether we respond to the income inequality we see with policies that help lift people up, or tear others down. The key to rising in this economy is skills—and the government's job is to make sure we have an education system that delivers them."[8]

The conservative disposition of Americans often rankles activists

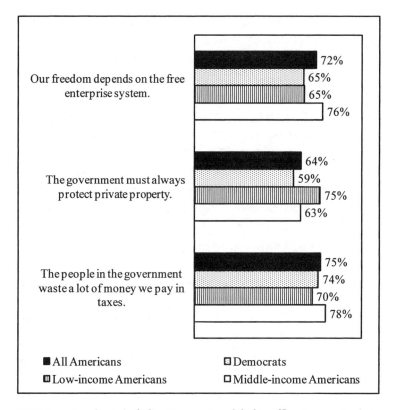

FIGURE 3.2 Americans, including Democrats and the less affluent, support private markets and distrust government in the abstract. Source: Inequality Survey.

on the Left, who find it disconcerting. Although opposition to specific reforms of "welfare" partly concerned how best to accomplish reforms, some hard-core opponents rejected the principle of linking welfare payments to work—a position that is out of step with the majority of Americans.

DISTRUST OF AND OPPOSITION TO GOVERNMENT. Americans' strong belief in individual self-reliance and in the potential for upward mobility coincides with deep-seated unease and distrust of government. A rather large minority of Americans (43 percent) even say that "most things would run pretty well by themselves if the government just didn't interfere," and this view has grown markedly since 1958, when only 25 percent embraced it.[9] Figure 3.2 showed that three-quarters of Americans, including large majorities of Democrats and low-income earners, say that people in the government waste a lot of money we pay in taxes. This sense of rampant government waste rose during the early 1970s and has stayed fairly high ever since, jumping even higher as the war in Iraq became costly and protracted.[10]

General distrust of government has also depressed public support for direct intervention to reduce economic inequality. Since at least 1987, pluralities or majorities of Americans have generally disagreed with the abstract proposition that it is the responsibility of government to reduce differences in income between people with high incomes and those with low incomes.[11]

Frustration with perceived government waste and incompetence pops up in communities around the country in letters to the editors of local newspapers. Ryan McQuighan pleaded in a letter to the *Baltimore Sun* to reject Governor O'Malley's proposal to raise revenues through slot machines and higher taxes. "Government spending never provides the most efficient solutions to problems. Why reward inefficiency with increasing funding?"[12]

Many Americans—like Walt Jankowski in New Jersey's Passaic County—see rampant government failure. "Our government has been broken for decades. It can't protect our borders. We have a 20th century military attempting to fight 21st century guerrillas. Things are only getting worse."[13]

Sue Metzger in Charleston, South Carolina, warned about relying on government to develop a comprehensive energy policy. "Although there is a clamor for government action, government solutions are nearly always worse than the problem."[14] Mark DeLuzio wrote to the *Hartford Courant,* connecting poor VA treatment of a wounded Iraq veteran to general government ineptitude. "We already have the evidence that federal government programs almost always miss their goals, and even though the free market has its problems, it is still more efficient and effective than the government will ever be."[15]

Pinched by the economic downturn, Michael Hoffman in Flint,

Michigan, tried to rally his neighbors to resist the false allure of government. "People need to wake up—they think they are voting for benefits, but they are only giving more money and control of their lives to the government. I urge everyone to vote no on every increase that comes up. . . . Governments have become an entity unto themselves, working to maintain themselves, their programs and their jobs and not working for the people."[16]

Frustration with perceived government incompetence and a philosophical inclination to encourage individual initiative fuel persistent calls by everyday Americans to resist the "nanny state" and the idea that "[people] are entitled to many benefits and they should be taken care of by the government. . . . The more the government gets involved, the problems get worse and the costs become greater."[17] John Legg in Tampa, Florida, informed his neighbors that "the solutions do not lay with another government program [but] . . . the community itself and the private sectors, churches and other nonprofit organizations of our community. . . . We need individual responsibility and family empowerment. . . . [T]ak[ing] the problems and solv[ing] them ourselves. . . . will make our communities stronger and ready to face its challenges."[18] A seventeen-year-old Tennessee high school senior concurred, reporting that "It is quite clear to my generation that the government is not the answer to our problems but indeed seems to be more and more at the root of our problems."[19]

The inclination of Americans (at least in the abstract) to prefer individual self-reliance and to doubt government competence may be propelled by a deep-seated sense that politicians are out of touch. Blair Erb in upstate New York echoed a common poll finding when she complained that "a persistent problem within our government and its representatives [is that] they are failing to listen to the people they represent."[20]

There is, then, a general conservatism in public opinion that embraces free enterprise, a connection between rewards and efforts, and skepticism about government. This conservative tilt is more apparent in the United States than in other modern democracies.

But pundits often misread—or perhaps deliberately distort—the public as being single-minded in hating government. For highbrow readers, *New York Times* columnist David Brooks claims that voters "don't believe government can lift their standard of living" and instead want a government that has a narrow "focus on a few macro threats" like terrorism.[21] Even respected scholars like Harvard professors Louis Hartz and Jennifer Hochschild have been read to suggest that Americans generally oppose government getting involved in how income and wealth are distributed.[22]

Jim Powell—a senior fellow at the Cato Institute, which promotes free markets and limited government—built a fan base by portraying FDR's New Deal policies as extending the Great Depression. *FDR's Folly* recycles seven decades of attacks (some of which are on the mark, some not) to make a larger point that resonates with a theme in American culture—namely, government ineptitude in contrast to the self-correcting ingenuity of markets and individuals.[23]

Highlighting and cheering on the public's antigovernment tendencies is hardly limited to the highbrow set. Best-selling author Michael Crichton widened his reach from sci-fi thrillers like *The Andromeda Strain* and *Jurassic Park* (and the popular television series *ER*) to pen a screed against a creeping takeover by government. *State of Fear* tells a harrowing tale of big-government types cleverly manipulating environmentalists to impose government control over the populace.

Like a cartoon, however, portrayals of Americans as uniformly conservative are mistaken. Objective evidence shows that the public's unease with government and its general deference to individuals coexists with strong, sustained public support for concrete government programs to extend opportunity and to ensure economic security where it is threatened. The truth is that the public's conservatism mostly operates at an abstract level. When Americans focus on the practical problems of everyday life, they look to government for help.

The Pragmatic Turn to Government

When Americans focus on threats to *economic security* or to the American Dream of *equal opportunity*, pragmatism often trumps abstract philosophy. Large majorities—majorities of both Republicans and Democrats, and majorities of high- as well as middle- and low-income earners—support government programs that moderate economic inequality by expanding opportunity and protecting Americans from harm. Our research reconfirms the early findings of Lloyd Free and Hadley Cantril, that Americans sound conservative when they express abstract, general sentiments, but are often liberal when it comes to specific social programs to help people.[24]

For example, seven out of ten of all Americans, including large majorities of Republicans and of the affluent, told us that they would *not* like to live in a society in which the government does nothing except provide national defense and police protection so that people would be left alone to earn whatever they could. About the same number said they believe that government "must see that no one is without food, clothing, or shelter." The idea of government-guaranteed food, clothing, and shelter has been favored by large majorities of Americans since at least 1964,[25] and is embraced across lines of class, race, and party. This is another example of public thinking that defies neat ideological pigeonholes. The public's pragmatic embrace of government is at odds with the often repeated and widely reported views of libertarians and small-government advocates.

Matthew Winschel wrote to the editor of the *St. Louis Post-Dispatch* to push back against virulent attacks on government. Although government may have its flaws, Winschel insisted that "society benefits when the government acts collectively to solve problems" such as illiteracy, premature death, and public-health disasters.[26]

OPPORTUNITY DOES NOT GROW ON TREES. Americans of all backgrounds almost unanimously embrace a core value—that everyone should have equal opportunity to make their way in the world. In our survey, 95 percent or more of Americans overall, of Republicans, and of the affluent agreed that "everyone in America should have equal opportunities to get ahead." Support for equal opportunity is so nearly universal that pollsters seldom bother to ask about it—we had to look back to 1957 to find the last time they did. But when they did ask, they found essentially the same thing. Five decades ago, 98 percent of Americans said that everyone should have equal opportunities.[27]

What, exactly, does "equal opportunity" mean? Does it mean that each American child at birth should have an exactly equal probability of achieving economic success? That would require drastic measures: generous compensation for deprived beginnings, and perhaps radical, direct redistribution by government of income and wealth so that all parents could provide equal environments for their children. Most Americans do not want to go that far. Instead they prefer a conservative approach that relies on rewarding the talent and hard work of individuals. The pragmatic spirit of Americans, though, fuses a belief in individual responsibility with the expectation that government will open up opportunities for education and for work.

The idea that government should empower individuals forms a foundation for both Democratic and Republican policies. President Bush's substantial expansion of federal government authority over elementary and secondary education, in defiance of his party's orthodoxy, was premised on the idea that large and growing federal government power was required in order to establish genuinely equal opportunity. Democratic policy makers like Clinton-administration economist Alan Blinder insist that "government action can make a difference, if done well," but accept the need to defer to individual performance within private markets: "Realistically, the underlying forces of the market are vastly stronger than anything the Government can do."[28]

EDUCATION AS THE GATEWAY TO OPPORTUNITY. Most Americans see education as the main gateway to equal opportunity. As figure 3.3 shows, large majorities of Americans overall, and majorities of those we often assume to be less supportive of government programs (Republicans and high-income earners), actually agree about government intervention in education.[29] Overwhelming majorities—more than eight out of ten—of all Americans, of Republicans, and of the affluent believe that the federal government should "spend whatever is necessary to ensure that all children have really

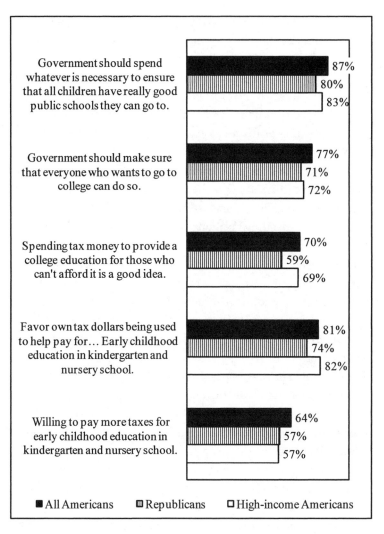

Government should spend whatever is necessary to ensure that all children have really good public schools they can go to.
87%
80%
83%

Government should make sure that everyone who wants to go to college can do so.
77%
71%
72%

Spending tax money to provide a college education for those who can't afford it is a good idea.
70%
59%
69%

Favor own tax dollars being used to help pay for... Early childhood education in kindergarten and nursery school.
81%
74%
82%

Willing to pay more taxes for early childhood education in kindergarten and nursery school.
64%
57%
57%

■ All Americans   ▥ Republicans   ▢ High-income Americans

FIGURE 3.3 Americans' broad agreement on supporting education. Source: Inequality Survey.

good public schools they can go to." This is not the position taken by some Republican elites in Washington. Who are they listening to?

Americans are willing to back up their preferences with their money. More than three-quarters of all Americans, of Republicans, and of the affluent come together to favor using their tax money to help pay for early-childhood education in kindergarten and nursery school. Majorities of all groups express willingness to pay *more* taxes for this purpose.

More than seven in ten of all Americans, of Republicans, and of high-income earners say that the federal government should make sure that everyone who wants to go to college can do so. More than six in ten say that spending tax money to provide a college education for those who can't afford it is a "good idea."

A consistent—but overlooked—theme is clear. Solid, and often very large, majorities of Republicans and the well-to-do—for whom cutting taxes is, according to some GOP elites, a sacred credo—say they are willing to devote their tax dollars or even pay *more* taxes to provide early-childhood education and college education for those who can't afford it. Why are the views of rank-and-file Republicans not represented in Washington by these GOP officials?

These majorities across different classes, races, and party loyalties—we can refer to them as "parallel majorities"—do not reflect an irresponsible "spend more on everything" mindset, heedless of taxes or tradeoffs. Americans do set priorities. Some six or more out of ten of all Americans, of Republicans, and of the affluent favor expanding aid to education (and to health care) rather than cutting it back or keeping it about the same. There is nearly as much support for increasing expenditures on Social Security. But far fewer Americans favor expanded spending on defense or foreign aid.[30]

The public's top priority has been clear and consistent for decades—expand government action to open up opportunity through education. And yet federal and state funding for early-childhood education falls short, locking out children who are eligible for Head Start and other preschool programs.[31] Inadequate spending on elementary through high schools has resulted in larger classes and inadequate instruction, and may contribute to high dropout rates. Federal spending to help people go to college with Pell Grants or other aid has fallen behind inflation and population growth. At the state level, post–high school education has become less affordable since the early 1990s, with forty-three states receiving "failing" grades in a recent evaluation.[32]

While more money is not the only ingredient for improving education and opening up opportunity, it is absolutely necessary. The public wants to provide it. Why don't the politicians in Washington and state capitols listen?

THE OPPORTUNITY TO WORK AND PAY YOUR OWN WAY. Americans favor individuals working their own way up rather than getting massive government handouts. They mean it. But they expect jobs and the ability to earn a living to actually be available.

Most Americans believe that work is a responsibility. The able-bodied *should* work. Americans have long opposed a "guaranteed income" regardless of work. They are split on providing generous benefits to the unemployed, out of fear that it would blunt incentives to find a new job.[33]

But for those who are ready to work, Americans view the opportunity to have a decent job as a *right* that the government should enforce. As figure 3.4 shows, some six out of ten of all Americans, of Republicans, and of higher-income earners believe that the government in Washington should "see to it" that everyone who wants to work can find a job. The large-majority support among all Americans is not new; it appears to date back at least half a century.[34] Remarkably, a narrow majority of Americans now actually support direct government hiring, despite widespread press coverage of politicians' calls for fewer government jobs. Most Americans—including half of all Republicans—now believe that the federal government should "*provide jobs*" for everyone able and willing to work but who cannot get a job in private employment.

Americans' pragmatism prompts them to strongly support two bulwarks for meaningful employment that reduce economic in-

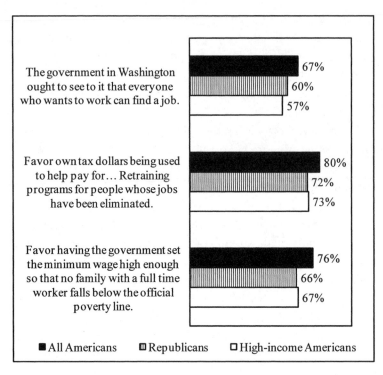

The government in Washington ought to see to it that everyone who wants to work can find a job.
67%
60%
57%

Favor own tax dollars being used to help pay for... Retraining programs for people whose jobs have been eliminated.
80%
72%
73%

Favor having the government set the minimum wage high enough so that no family with a full time worker falls below the official poverty line.
76%
66%
67%

■ All Americans   ◫ Republicans   ☐ High-income Americans

FIGURE 3.4 Americans support government help with jobs and wages. Source: Inequality Survey.

equality by enabling individuals to advance themselves. The first is job training. Three-quarters or more of all Americans, of Republicans, and of the affluent favor using their tax dollars to help pay for retraining people whose jobs have been eliminated. Even after our interviewees were told that some people say federal retraining programs "just create big government programs that do not work very well," solid majorities of all Americans and of the affluent still favored more government investment in worker retraining and education to help workers adapt to changes in the economy. Majorities of the public have felt this way at least since 1999.[35]

A second bulwark for meaningful employment is having the government help ensure that work pays. More than two-thirds of all Americans, Republicans, and high-income Americans favor having the government set the minimum wage high enough so that no family with a full-time worker falls below the official poverty line. This view is bolstered by new research debunking assertions that the minimum wage just causes unemployment.[36]

The American public also supports a program presidents Ronald Reagan and Bill Clinton expanded that helps low-income working families by reducing their income taxes or giving them refunds, a program known officially as the Earned Income Tax Credit (EITC). About half of all Americans (48 percent) want to increase help from the EITC; only 5 percent want to decrease it. More than six out of ten of all Americans, of Republicans, and of the affluent favor expanding this program to cover workers who are single, rather than only those with families (as is the case in the current program).

In our era of downsizing, outsourcing, mass layoffs, stagnant wages, and rising prices, many Americans are afraid that they or other Americans may lose their jobs and not find new ones while bills mount.[37]

Americans across parties, races, classes, and income levels come together behind the principle that everyone should work to make ends meet and that government should make sure they can do so. The much-ballyhooed class and partisan warfare is hard to find in our communities around the country.

Government Help with Security against Illness or Poverty

Americans prefer that individuals support themselves through their own hard work. They realize, though, that forces beyond the control of any individual may intervene. When people are faced with threats to their ability to earn a living, Americans favor government intervention—including intervention to help secure health care, respectable retirement pensions, and relief from deep poverty.

ENSURING HEALTH TO PURSUE OPPORTUNITY. Many Americans are not healthy enough to take advantage of the opportunities available in our society. American girls are born with a life expectancy that ranks nineteenth in the world. Male babies rank thirty-first—in a dead tie with Belize and Dar es Salaam. American men live only as long as men in the State of Brunei. Among the wealthiest countries, the United States ranks poorly on almost every measure of health, including infant mortality, low birth weight, life expectancy at birth, and life expectancy for infants. The average American boy lives three and a half years less long than the average Japanese baby, even though the Japanese child is a lot more likely to grow up smoking cigarettes. The American adolescent death rate is two-thirds higher than, say, England's.[38]

Americans' dismal average performance on the world stage masks vast differences across our population. Asian American women live over twenty years longer than black males dwelling in violent urban areas, who have life expectancies resembling those found in the poorest countries in the world like Belarus and Uzbekistan. A male born in some sections of Washington, D.C., has a life expectancy thirteen years shorter than a woman born in rural Minnesota (sixty-eight years versus eighty-one years).[39] This hardly squares with equal opportunity.

Tragic differences in health stem, in part, from the failure to insure some forty-seven million men, women, and children—16 percent of the population. Fifty-seven to fifty-nine million lack insurance at some point during the year, according to the nonpartisan Congressional Budget Office. Perhaps thirty million are underinsured, meaning that their insurance fails to cover their medical costs.[40]

The bottom line has been well established by our leading doctors and scientists: lack of adequate and consistent health insurance translates into poor health, which hobbles individuals from pursuing the American Dream. Simple medical care—annual checkups, screenings, vaccinations, eyeglasses, dentistry—saves lives and improves well-being, but its availability is shockingly uneven. Well-insured people get assigned hospital beds; the uninsured get patched up and sent back to the streets. From diagnostic procedures (prostate screenings, mammograms, pap smears) to treatment for asthma, the uninsured get less care. They get it later in their illnesses. They are roughly three times more likely to have an adverse health outcome. The Institute of Medicine blames gaps in insurance coverage for seventeen thousand preventable deaths a year.[41] These are facts, not ideology. Most Americans may not know the statistical details, but they understand the basic idea that health insurance is necessary to pursue opportunity. The former backbone of American health insurance—employer-sponsored coverage—has rapidly eroded, with its reach declining from 68 percent of the nonelderly population to 62 percent in just the seven years between 2000 and 2006. This impacted nearly six million Americans.[42]

The uninsured and underinsured look to government for help. As figure 3.5 shows, substantial majorities of Americans overall, of Republicans, and of the affluent expect the federal government and/ or "all employers"—presumably mandated by government—to take responsibility for ensuring that everyone has health insurance. (Interestingly, somewhat larger majorities of Republicans support an employer-based system, while more high-income earners would prefer the direct government route.) Overall, three-quarters of Americans have consistently supported expansion of federal government health-care programs since at least 1994, and growing majorities have supported the government taking responsibility for everyone having health coverage.[43]

Although warnings against "socialized medicine" may have blinded some politicians and pundits to what Americans actually prefer, there is broad agreement across partisan and income groupings that the government should bring about universal health insurance coverage. Any of several different approaches would do. Today nearly two-thirds of all Americans, a majority of high-income earners, and nearly half of Republicans favor the establishment of "national health insurance, financed by tax money, that would pay for most forms of health care." Large majority support for this policy has been found in eleven separate polls since 1980, and the level of support has risen since 2000.[44] According to a separate question, seven

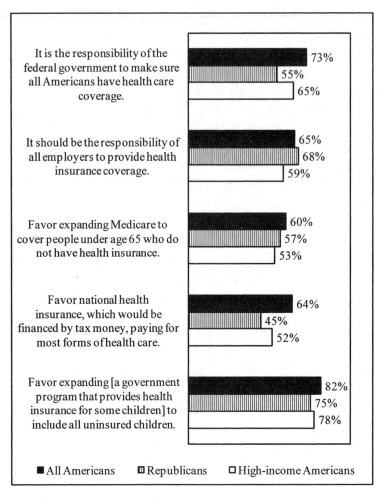

It is the responsibility of the federal government to make sure all Americans have health care coverage.
73%
55%
65%

It should be the responsibility of all employers to provide health insurance coverage.
65%
68%
59%

Favor expanding Medicare to cover people under age 65 who do not have health insurance.
60%
57%
53%

Favor national health insurance, which would be financed by tax money, paying for most forms of health care.
64%
45%
52%

Favor expanding [a government program that provides health insurance for some children] to include all uninsured children.
82%
75%
78%

■ All Americans   ▥ Republicans   ☐ High-income Americans

FIGURE 3.5 Americans support government help with health insurance. Source: Inequality Survey.

out of ten of all Americans, and half or more of Republicans and of the affluent, say they favor using their tax dollars to provide health coverage for everyone.

Most striking is that a majority of Americans (54 percent)—including just under half of Republicans and of the affluent (45 percent and 49 percent, respectively)—now strongly or somewhat favor what generations of reform opponents have treated as the Great Satan of health care: "a national health plan, financed by the taxpayers, in which all Americans would get their insurance from a single government plan." This is new.[45]

A more popular alternative, however, is to expand the existing, highly esteemed government program that now provides health insurance to the elderly. Sixty percent of Americans overall, and majorities of Republicans and of the affluent, favor expanding Medicare to cover the uninsured under age sixty-five, a level of overall support that has persisted at least since 1999.[46]

More than three-quarters of all Americans, of Republicans, and of the affluent favor expanding another established government program—the State Child Health Insurance Program, or SCHIP—in order to cover all children who are currently uninsured. In October 2007, President Bush vetoed bipartisan congressional legislation that would have moderately broadened the program, leading conservative Utah Republican Orrin Hatch to declare bluntly that "some have given the president bad advice . . . [because expanding coverage to] children is the morally right thing to do."[47]

Although some Republican officials and Washington insiders scorn proposals for expanding government responsibility for health insurance, the truth is that rank-and-file Republicans around the country do want government action to move toward universal coverage. Conversely, advocates of single-payer health systems may overreach the views of most Americans (including Democrats and the less affluent), given their distrust of government and the satisfaction of many with current private medical care. Successful reform of health care will likely require a pragmatic approach that incrementally expands existing programs to address unmet needs and rising costs without offending Americans' conservatism.[48]

WORK HARD AND RETIRE WITH DIGNITY. Americans of all backgrounds expect seniors, after spending most of a lifetime working, to be able to retire with dignity and economic security. Well into the 1900s, most people worked until physical decline made it impossible and then they relied on family, friends, neighbors, or local charity. But the idea that "the community" should support seniors is now rejected by six out of ten Americans overall (as it was already rejected back in 1958[49]) and by majorities of Republicans and the affluent (see fig. 3.6). Backing for a more organized system to support seniors in retirement stems from respect for a lifetime of work as well as from self-preservation: families struggling to provide for themselves cannot afford the cost of supporting their parents.[50]

As in the case of health insurance, Americans are open to more than one approach to providing decent incomes to retirees. Employer-based pensions are one. As figure 3.6 shows, substantial majorities of all Americans, including majorities of Republicans and the affluent, believe that it should be the responsibility of all employers to provide retirement benefits coverage. Although employer-based programs could do this job in theory, only half or fewer of Americans are now actually covered by their employers.[51] Even well-established programs have vanished in bankruptcies and downsizing. Half of all seniors, and millions of those with disabilities, would fall into poverty if left to rely solely on what employers now offer or on their savings.[52] To ensure that this private-sector option would actually cover all employees, therefore, would probably require a government mandate that employers must do so.

Another approach supported by large majorities of Americans involves direct government provision of retirement pensions. Confronted with the stark prospect of poverty in older age, most Americans count on Social Security for a minimal level of support. They favor Social Security even if it means shifting some income from the better-off—hardly a message that we hear in today's polarized debates in Washington. Solid majorities of all Americans, of Republicans, and of the affluent want Social Security to ensure a minimum standard of living to all contributors even if some receive benefits exceeding the value of their contributions (as is often the case among lower-income workers). A majority of Americans already felt this way back in 1998.[53]

More than half of all Americans and of Republicans, and nearly half of the affluent, favor *expanding* Social Security; the rest mostly

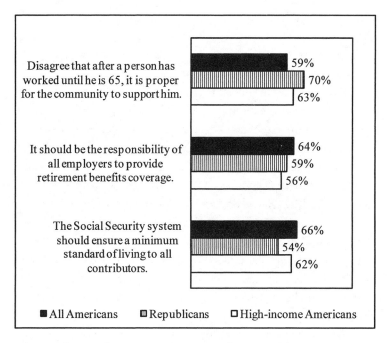

Disagree that after a person has worked until he is 65, it is proper for the community to support him.
59%
70%
63%

It should be the responsibility of all employers to provide retirement benefits coverage.
64%
59%
56%

The Social Security system should ensure a minimum standard of living to all contributors.
66%
54%
62%

■ All Americans   ⊞ Republicans   ☐ High-income Americans

FIGURE 3.6 Support for government provision of minimum income in retirement. Source: Inequality Survey.

want to keep it the same. Hardly anyone wants to cut it back. Decades of polling have shown similar majorities in favor of expanding Social Security, as well as large and persistent opposition to reducing benefits by cutting cost-of-living adjustments, raising the retirement age, or taxing payments more heavily.[54] Broad public support for maintaining and expanding Social Security has held up in the face of tireless campaigns to reduce benefits by elite pressure groups like the well-funded Concord Coalition.

Loyalty to Social Security bubbles up all over the country. Seventy-six-year-old Shirley Stedman of Michigan gushed that "the government is doing a good job" with the program.[55] Morton Parsons from upstate New York agreed; in a letter to a Syracuse editor he described Social Security as "one of the most successful programs ever established by the federal government."[56] John Alaria, Sr., from Kincaid,

Illinois, complained that he is "tired of hearing people can handle their money better than the government can. . . . For most people, they would never be able to save enough money to draw a monthly check equivalent to their Social Security."[57]

Although critics of Social Security try to scare Americans with overblown talk of the program's "crisis" and imminent bankruptcy, the public supports modest adjustments that continue to offer a proven path forward—one that has produced trust-fund surpluses for decades in the past. Half or more of all Americans, of Republicans, and of the affluent support several specific steps to ensure the future financial health of Social Security. One would be to allow benefits to grow more slowly for middle- and high-income people while allowing the benefits to grow as scheduled for low-income people. A still more popular step, which experts say could wipe out the entire projected shortfall in the Social Security trust fund over the next seventy-five years,[58] would be to raise or eliminate the "cap" on income subject to the payroll tax. A solid majority of Americans favor doing so.[59] (As of 2007, taxes were paid only on the first $97,500 of earned wages, shielding the more affluent Americans from being taxed on most of their salaries and totally excluding income from stock-market profits or gains from other investments.)

Yet again we discover that majorities of everyday Republicans and of the affluent favor a tax increase: subjecting higher incomes to payroll taxes. This violates self-interest; the rich would have to pay more. Contrary to simple economic models of self-interested human behavior, however, both Republicans and affluent Americans put the soundness of the Social Security system, and its protection of the less fortunate, above their own narrow economic self-interest. Meanwhile some GOP politicians in Washington and their hired guns denounce these very proposals as unthinkable violations of "their" party's principles. Whose party is it?

HELPING THE POOR, WHEN ALL ELSE FAILS. Americans prefer that individuals make it on their own. They oppose guaranteed income without work for those who are not old or physically disabled.[60] They are also socially conservative, disliking childbearing by single mothers and especially by teenagers.

Nonetheless, Americans do support government assistance when people fall into poverty, which happens more often in the United States than in any other advanced industrialized country. More than one in ten Americans—thirty-six million people—are poor, with 40 percent classified as "severely poor" by the U.S. Census because they fail to make it even halfway to the poverty line. Many of the poor are children, who, through no fault of their own, face tremendous obstacles to pursuing the American Dream unless they get government help.[61]

Most Americans realize that poverty seldom results from laziness. Their instinct is to be generous. A majority of Americans (though not of Republicans) disagree with the stereotype that "many poor people simply don't want to work hard." Nearly all Americans, including nearly all Republicans and higher-income citizens, agree that one should always find ways to help others less fortunate than oneself (see fig. 3.7).

More than six out of ten of all Americans, of Republicans, and of the affluent want government to see that no one is without life's basic necessities—food, clothing, or shelter. Still larger majorities favor using their tax dollars to help pay for food stamps and other assistance to the poor. Remarkably, despite widespread opposition to welfare and a general aversion to out-of-wedlock pregnancies, two-thirds of all Americans, of Republicans, and of the affluent support their tax dollars being used to pay for "welfare benefits for the children of single teenage mothers."

Agreement on antipoverty measures—like all the other policy areas we have considered—cuts across lines of race as well as class. The propositions that "government must see that no one is without food, clothing, or shelter" and that respondents' own tax dollars should be used "to help pay for food stamps and other assistance to the poor" were supported by very large majorities of whites, nonwhites, low-income whites, and unskilled white workers,[62] as well as by Republicans, Democrats, the middle class, and the more affluent.

71

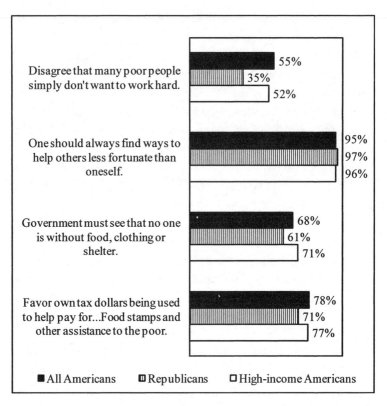

Disagree that many poor people
simply don't want to work hard.
— 55%
— 35%
— 52%

One should always find ways to
help others less fortunate than
oneself.
— 95%
— 97%
— 96%

Government must see that no one
is without food, clothing or
shelter.
— 68%
— 61%
— 71%

Favor own tax dollars being used
to help pay for...Food stamps and
other assistance to the poor.
— 78%
— 71%
— 77%

■ All Americans   ▥ Republicans   ▢ High-income Americans

FIGURE 3.7 Support for government assistance for the poor. Source: Inequality Survey.

Yet again the bitter attacks by pundits and politicians stand in stark contrast to the convictions of majorities of rank-and-file Republicans and high-income earners, who support government help for the poor and are willing to devote their tax dollars to get the job done. This points toward the existence of a new silent majority.

The New Silent Majority

Ordinary Americans want a society in which individuals have genuine opportunities to move up economically. They resist proposals for massive, direct government programs that would redistribute income and wealth by taking them from the rich. This is a conservative view of the world, one that is buttressed by deep-seated suspicion and unease regarding the competence and integrity of government.

Yet Americans are also pragmatic in sizing up the actual operation of our society. They expect individuals to take care of themselves, but they accept that government help may be needed to address concrete barriers to pursuing opportunity. Our new survey confirms a conclusion based on years of previous research: large majorities of Americans favor programs that equip individuals to pursue employment opportunities through education and training, and programs that protect them from threats to economic security such as illness, old age, or disability.

America's unique blend of philosophical conservatism and operational liberalism leads to a particular approach to addressing economic inequality, *conservative egalitarianism*. Enabling more Americans to pursue opportunities for lifting themselves up, and better securing them from disasters, would greatly diminish today's extreme concentration of income and wealth without confiscation from the rich.

To listen to the squabbling in Washington, one might think that around the country Republicans are fighting Democrats and the rich are fighting lower-income earners. Not so. In contrast to the nasty combat among pundits and politicians, ordinary Americans are not engaged in partisan war or class war.

There is, in fact, a new silent majority. A consensus exists across parties and across income groupings that individuals ought to do their best to care for themselves, but that government ought to foster opportunities and protect individuals against threats that might impede their actual exercise of opportunity.

Majorities of Republicans as well as Democrats and independents, and majorities of high-income as well as middle- and lower-income Americans, favor a wide range of egalitarian government programs. Programs to ensure that all Americans can get an education that equips them to make their own way in the world; to help them find rewarding jobs rather than slipping into poverty; to keep them healthy and productive; and to secure their dignity in retirement by providing a minimum income. Although Americans at different income levels and with different party loyalties of course disagree about some matters, the most striking point—a largely neglected point—is their majority agreement in favor of such policies.[63]

Republican and Democratic officials in Washington have not always heeded the voice of the American public or even the voice of their own rank and file. Democratic politicians who resisted connecting welfare to work were out of step with most Americans, including rank-and-file Democrats, who expect individuals to support themselves and oppose a guaranteed income. Republican elites in Washington have not spoken for everyday Republicans when they have denounced government as "the problem," opposed investments in education and worker retraining, fought against increases in the minimum wage, or resisted steps to expand access to health insurance. It seems time for the new silent majority to be heard in Washington.

We now turn to another area of surprisingly broad agreement across class and party lines: taxes.

4

Paying the Bill

"All right," a critic may say, "you have shown that Americans favor government programs that would enhance opportunity and reduce inequality. But are they willing to pay for those programs? Will they bear the tax burden?" If not, this is all just pie in the sky.

And what do Americans think about particular *kinds* of taxes? If they favored regressive taxes that hit low-income people hardest, programs to expand opportunity and ensure economic security might be nullified.

The Anti-Tax Cliché

There are well-organized efforts in Washington and state capitals to relentlessly promote tax cuts and resist any talk of tax increases. The organizations go by different names, but their mission is similar. The Club for Growth and Grover Norquist's Americans for Tax Reform are active in Washington, while state groups include various

Taxpayer Associations and Taxpayer Leagues as well as innocuous-sounding "Policy Research Institutes." Mostly funded by large corporations and wealthy individuals, they sound tax-hike alarms, campaign against taxes, lobby politicians, and warn wavering officials with threats of punishment at the polls.

Anti-tax zealots even bashed Republican President George H. W. Bush for accepting a small tax increase that Congress had initiated, an increase that helped set the stage for the budget surpluses of the Clinton years. Republican governors, including such conservatives as Mike Huckabee (Arkansas), Mitch Daniels (Indiana), and Tim Pawlenty (Minnesota), have been lambasted for agreeing to increased taxes or fees—even when ordered by courts to do so and when overwhelming legislative majorities demanded the new revenue.

One tactic of the anti-tax campaigners is to craft poll-tested words and arguments that resonate with Americans, providing potent weapons to attack proposed tax increases. Fox News host Bill O'Reilly, for instance, charged that New Jersey was "stealing" from the rich to give to the poor by proposing to raise taxes on incomes over $500,000 to give property-tax relief to lower-income people: "That's communism, that's socialism."[1] Former House majority leader Richard Armey (R-TX, known as "The Hammer") declared that the tax code has been "corrupted" for purposes like income redistribution that are "not legitimate." "The American definition of fairness," Armey explained, is treating "everyone . . . exactly as everyone else"—apparently meaning that the rich should not have to pay more.[2] The *Wall Street Journal* ran a series of editorials denouncing President Bill Clinton's mild tax increases on the affluent under the headline "The Class Warfare Economy," with a graphic of a guillotine.[3]

Criticism of taxes is often pitched in populist terms that pit underdog Davids against a huge Goliath of government that wants to confiscate earnings and oppress the "little people." A letter to the newspaper editor in Flint, Michigan, echoed this message: Michael Hoffman alerted his neighbors that the state legislature's decision to "rais[e] our taxes" meant that "we are trapped . . . [and] government . . . is putting the squeeze on us."[4]

The Public's Conservative Streak

The organized resistance to taxes resonates with a genuine philosophical conservativism among many Americans.

GOVERNMENT WASTE. One source of public unease with taxes stems from distrust of government and suspicion that it engages in rampant waste, fraud, and abuse. Figure 4.1 shows that substantial majorities since 1968 have generally said that the government wastes "a lot" of the money we pay in taxes (with a sharp decline, however, following the Clinton balanced-budget period of the later 1990s, and a temporary drop below 50 percent after the 9/11 attacks).[5] Who wants to pay taxes for programs that are wasteful, unnecessary, or even harmful?

DOUBTS ABOUT FAIRNESS. Distrust of government's ability to spend wisely or well teams up with a deep suspicion about the fair-

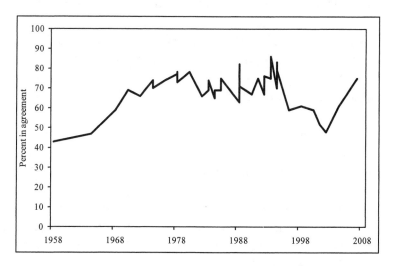

FIGURE 4.1 Government wastes "a lot" of tax money. Source: NES, CBS/*New York Times*, Gallup, Market Strategies, *Washington Post*/ABC, and Inequality Survey. "Do you think that people in the government waste a lot of money we pay in taxes, waste some of it, or don't waste very much of it?"

ness of the tax system. Durable majorities of Americans regularly conclude that *their own* income taxes are too high.[6] They suspect that others (especially the rich) find sneaky ways to avoid paying their fair share. Pundits and politicians from across the spectrum have attempted to respond.

O'Reilly, Armey, and others tap into the public's worry about tax fairness when they fend off proposals to tax higher-income groups and businesses; they try to transmute resentment of loopholes into resentment of taxes generally. The irony is that some who warn everyday Americans about unfairness are also the strongest proponents of tax cuts that favor the most affluent.

From the other side of the political spectrum, Democratic politicians have raised quite different concerns about fairness. During the 2008 presidential campaign, Barack Obama charged at a Nashua, New Hampshire, restaurant that "special interests in Washington have carved out a trillion dollars worth of corporate tax loopholes." He told Joe the Plumber that "when you spread the wealth around, it's good for everybody."[7] John Edwards declared in North Carolina that it is "time to restore fairness to a tax code that has been driven badly out of whack by the wrongheaded rules of the Washington establishment—more wealth for the wealthy and more power for the powerful." "The middle-class," Edwards declared, "shouldn't pay higher taxes than when the rich make money from money."[8]

WIDESPREAD CONFUSION ABOUT TAXES. Americans' unease about or resistance to taxes also reflects confusion about how different kinds of taxes work and which taxes would be best for themselves and the country. In contrast to European tax systems, which rely on the concealed value-added tax, U.S. taxes are highly visible, yet the tax code is extremely complicated and hard to understand.[9] Confusion is particularly widespread among lower-income people. Anti-tax crusaders have sometimes taken advantage of that confusion or deliberately cultivated it.

Take the personal income tax, a major source of funding for federal government programs. In the Inequality Survey, we found that fewer than one-third (only 31 percent) of low-income earners realize that the personal income tax lands more heavily on higher-income people than on themselves. Forty-three percent mistakenly believe that *lower*-income people pay a higher percentage of what they earn for income taxes. But most of the affluent (54 percent) understand full well who pays; only 33 percent say that lower-income people do.[10] The combination of confusion among the less affluent about who bears the burden of personal income taxes, with clarity among higher-income groups, helps make this tax unpopular and politically vulnerable. We found that it ranks as the second most unpopular tax for the government to use "a lot" for generating revenue to fund government programs.[11]

Not only do many of the less well-off fail to understand that the income tax is favorable to them, but most Americans of all income levels fail to perceive the heavy burden that sales taxes put on working people and their families. The great majority of Americans flunk this tax quiz: they incorrectly believe that all income groups pay about the same or that *higher*-income people pay a greater percentage of what they earn in sales taxes. Only one-fifth of Americans correctly understand that lower-income folks pay more.

The facts are agreed upon by all respected economists: sales and excise taxes fall most heavily on lower-income people. They are therefore referred to as "regressive" taxes. The key is that these taxes are "flat"—meaning that the same rate (say, 7 or 8 percent) is paid by everyone making a purchase. But lower-income people have to spend a larger share of their incomes on necessities subject to sales taxes, so that sales taxes take away a higher proportion of their incomes. Paying $80 (including taxes) every week or two to fill the car with gas does not bother a pair of affluent lawyers who pull in ten grand a week, but it really hurts a family struggling to get by on $300 or $400 a week.

The opposite of regressive taxes are "progressive" taxes like the personal income tax, which take higher proportions of income from the more affluent. For instance, an investment banker might pay 20 or 30 percent in income taxes on $1,000,000 of salary and bonuses, versus the 10 percent or so that a working family might pay on $50,000 in wages. But of course the investment banker would be left with much more after taxes.

Confusion and misunderstanding haunts public attitudes about other taxes as well. Only 39 percent of Americans realize that property taxes take a bigger percentage of what higher-income people earn than they take from those with lower incomes. (Economists nearly all agree that property taxes mostly fall on the owners of real property or on the owners of capital in general.)

For two important taxes there is somewhat more clarity. Nearly half of all Americans (46 percent) perceive that corporate income taxes are paid more by higher-income than by lower-income people; only 22 percent think that lower-income people pay a greater percentage of their earnings in corporate income taxes. Similarly, many Americans (39 percent) realize that *lower*-income people pay more of their earnings in payroll taxes; only 25 percent think the opposite. The payroll taxes that fund Social Security and Medicare are quite visible; wage earners can see FICA deductions right on their pay stubs. We will see that relative clarity about the incidence of corporate income and payroll taxes are reflected in policy preferences. There is much more support for corporate income taxes than for payroll taxes.

Still, substantial numbers of Americans are confused even about who pays the payroll and corporate income taxes. Moreover, almost two-thirds of Americans fail to realize that our country has nearly the lowest overall tax rates among twenty-five economically developed countries.[12] The Inequality Survey found that more than a quarter of the public mistakenly thought that Americans pay a *higher* proportion of their income in taxes than European countries do, and an additional third or so erroneously imagined the rates to be similar or confessed they did not know. Several previous polls have found much the same thing.[13]

Research experiments indicate that providing individuals with more information about who benefits from various tax provisions has an impact on their policy preferences. Explaining that the tax deduction for home mortgages most benefits households with annual earnings of $100,000 or more tended to reduce support for this deduction among the less affluent.[14] Such findings suggest that public views that conflict with their interests may stem from a lack of accessible and accurate information—which in turn may reflect the obscurity and technical complexity of the U.S. tax code, as well as misleading or deceptive rhetoric from politicians and others—rather than from cognitive limitations of individuals.[15]

Willingness to Pay Taxes for Important Government Programs

Although Americans embrace individual liberty, free enterprise, and small government, and although many may be misled by incomplete or inaccurate information about taxes, most Americans are also mature enough to understand that taxes have to be paid in order to fund government programs that create opportunity or provide security for individuals against threats beyond their control. Our own research, as well as that of others, demonstrates that there is surprisingly little public sentiment in favor of general tax cuts. Most Americans would actually accept tax *increases* for certain purposes. Moreover, the public endorses progressive taxes—that is, taxes that fall more heavily on those most able to afford them.

And there is remarkable consensus across parties, classes, races, and other categories of Americans. Majorities or pluralities of Republicans as well as Democrats, and of upper- and middle-income Americans as well as low-income people, agree about most of these matters. Pitched battles among politicians, pundits, and pressure groups obscure this remarkable level of agreement within the American public.

USING TAXES FOR PRAGMATIC EGALITARIAN PROGRAMS. Very large majorities of Americans favor their tax dollars being used to help pay for a range of government programs that would enhance equal opportunity or provide economic security. Figure 4.2 shows that supermajorities of 70 percent up to 81 percent favor their taxes being used for early-childhood education in kindergarten and nurs-

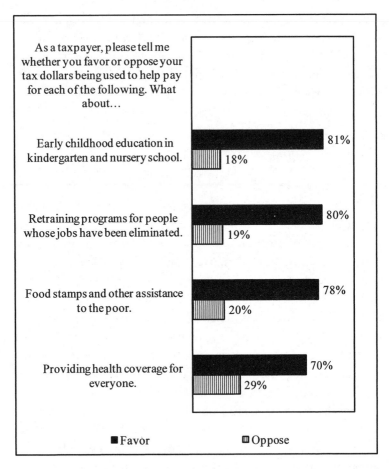

As a taxpayer, please tell me whether you favor or oppose your tax dollars being used to help pay for each of the following. What about...

Early childhood education in kindergarten and nursery school.
81%
18%

Retraining programs for people whose jobs have been eliminated.
80%
19%

Food stamps and other assistance to the poor.
78%
20%

Providing health coverage for everyone.
70%
29%

■ Favor   ▥ Oppose

FIGURE 4.2 The public supports using tax dollars for concrete programs. Source: Inequality Survey.

ery school, for worker retraining, for assistance to the poor, and for providing health-care coverage to everyone. (Not shown: two-thirds even favor using their tax dollars to help pay for welfare benefits for the children of single teenage mothers, long a target of criticism.)

Americans are realists. They recognize that important government programs must be paid for.

Americans also make distinctions, preferring to target the use of their tax dollars on what they see as the highest priorities. We found that the level of support for committing tax dollars to early-childhood education, worker retraining, and assisting the poor is about the same as for funding defense and military programs. By contrast, using tax money to pay for public broadcasting and the arts, or for economic aid to other countries, enjoys far less support—only about half as much.[16]

TAX INCREASES IF NECESSARY. Despite all the noisy rhetoric, there is in fact surprisingly little public support for cutting taxes. When we asked in general terms whether people thought that taxes should be increased, decreased, or kept about the same, there was no sign of tax-cutting mania. Fewer than one-third favored decreasing taxes, compared to the two-thirds that preferred to keep them at the same level or increase them.

Indeed, Americans not only support directing their current tax dollars to valued government programs, but most also accept the need to pay *more* taxes for specific purposes. About six out of ten Americans express willingness to pay higher taxes in order to provide health coverage for everyone, or for early-childhood education in kindergarten and nursery school.

Many Americans support a variety of local taxes to support specific programs, especially education. "As much as I don't like paying taxes," a resident of Napa County, California, confesses, "we need to do Measure G [for] the poor kids in American Canyon—I can't imagine my kids doing a three-and-a-half-hour commute each day just to go to school." Another realist spoke up in Guilford County, North Carolina: "I hate paying taxes. But the fact of the matter is, they're what build schools." This pragmatic acceptance of taxes to pay for essentials percolates up all over the country. In South Bend, Indiana: "I don't like to pay taxes more than anyone else, but if we don't educate our kids, how are we going to compete?" San Antonio, Texas: "The growth is just tremendous. We need more schools. I hate to pay the taxes, but I'm agreeing to it." Spokane, Washington: "Good Lord, I don't like to pay taxes either, but I like my services. I've gotten used to having my street plowed and seeing a police vehicle here and there."[17]

Public acceptance of increased taxes to pay for services may seem astounding in an era marked by anti-tax rhetoric and by a series of deep cuts in federal taxes. But it is a real feature of the American scene, a feature that has often been obscured or ignored. Here's another.

HIGHER TAXES ON THE MORE AFFLUENT. Taxes that fall more heavily on the more affluent (that is, "progressive" taxes) have been a particular target of political attacks. There is plenty of conflict about this among pundits and Washington politicians, but there is remarkable agreement among ordinary Americans, including most of the affluent themselves.

Hard-nosed business man and multibillionaire Warren Buffett, for example, sets aside his selfish interests. He agrees that "class warfare" has broken out, but gives a very different interpretation of it from the usual: "It's class warfare. My class is winning, but they shouldn't be."[18] Bill Gates, Sr. (yes, the father of the Microsoft titan), slaps down claims that the super rich "earned" their wealth and therefore should keep it: "you earned it with the indispensable help of your government" with education, infrastructure, and research—including the Internet and biotechnology. This should foster an attitude of "gratitude and recognition of our obligation to pass on similar opportunities."[19]

Buffett and Gates are not alone. Over two thousand of the richest Americans—including Bill Gates, Jr., David Rockefeller, Jr., and George Soros—have called for keeping an important type of progressive tax, the estate tax.[20]

A historical note: despite contemporary disputes, the policy that the rich should pay more taxes is neither a recent notion nor a conspiracy hatched by extreme liberals. It was supported by Republican presidents Theodore Roosevelt and William Taft, who backed the constitutional amendment that permitted a progressive personal income tax in 1913.[21]

Leaders in both political parties, as well as many of the super rich like Buffet, Gates, and Rockefeller, recognize that the affluent can pay more in taxes—helping to fund government services needed for a skilled, competitive, and reasonably contented workforce—while still holding on to vast fortunes.

Consider this imaginary scenario involving one of the hedge-fund managers who took in more than $1 billion in a single year. If he had to pay a 40 percent income tax on his one billion dollars, that would yield $400 million to help pay for defense, healthcare, education, and the like. Yet he would still have a comfortable $600 million left to save or spend as he wished. A mere mortal might pay taxes at a much lower rate of 10 percent on a $50,000 salary, but struggle to support a family with the $45,000 that was left over. The rich can pay more and still do very well. This is the argument made by Buffet, Gates, and other members of the super-rich club.

We called the above scenario "imaginary" because the progressivity of taxes has been eroded away in recent years. Even beyond general income tax cuts for the affluent, hedge-fund managers get a special tax break: they can call most of their income "capital gains." So they generally pay taxes at about the same low rate (around 15 percent) as secretaries or shirt salesmen.[22] But the point remains: the super rich *could* pay more.

Majorities of Americans side with Buffet and Gates in supporting the general principle of progressive taxation. They also favor using specific types of taxes that fall harder on those who are most able to pay.

Fifty-four percent of Americans said in our survey that people with high incomes should pay a larger or much larger share of their income in taxes than those with low incomes. (Similar results have been found in other polls since 1987.)[23] Fifty-six percent said the government should redistribute wealth by heavy taxes on the rich. Figure 4.3 shows that support for redistribution through heavy taxes on the rich has increased markedly over the last seventy years and appears to have reached a record high.[24]

The public's belief that taxes should land harder on the more affluent goes beyond a vague generalization. It extends to support for two

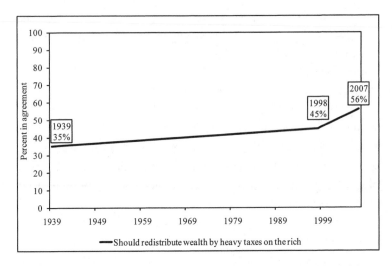

FIGURE 4.3 Support for government redistributing wealth by taxing the rich heavily. Source: Roper for *Fortune*, March 1939; Gallup for GM, April–May, 1998; Gallup, April 2007; Inequality Survey, 2007.

specific types of progressive revenue raisers—estate taxes and corporate income taxes—and for raising or eliminating the regressive cap on payroll taxes.

Despite all the fuss about opposition to the "death tax," it turns out that only 14 percent of Americans (14 percent!) agree with proposals to altogether abolish the estate tax. Given a choice of possible rates including zero, the average American favors a tax of about 25 percent on estates worth $100 million or more—not far from the actual level of the tax.[25] Previous polls have also found large majorities in support of the estate tax (even when it is pejoratively described as the "death tax"), especially if reforms shield small businesses, family farms, and ordinary taxpayers. Some anti-taxers have tried to make it look as if a majority favored repeal of the tax; for instance, Frank Luntz jerry-rigged his results by combining the modest 35 percent who said they favored abolishing the estate tax with the 50 percent who favored keeping the tax but reforming it.[26]

Fact check: the estate tax now applies only to very large estates left by the rich—as of 2009, only to the fraction of 1 percent of estates valued at more than $3.5 million. It has generated a whopping $1 trillion of revenue in a decade that would otherwise have had to come from middle- and upper-middle earners. Charges that the "death tax" forces the sale of long-held family farms or family-built small businesses have been contradicted by careful investigations. Current law exempts from the estate tax all but the very largest estates.

The public also favors making payroll taxes less regressive. A solid majority of Americans (58 percent) in 2007 wanted to raise the (then about $97,000) cap on income subject to the payroll tax; only 6 percent wanted to lower it. By increasing taxes on the highest income earners, this would have a very progressive effect on the U.S. tax system.

A progressive tax that Americans strongly favor is the corporate income tax, which a plurality of people see as paid more heavily by those with higher incomes. Six out of ten Americans single out this tax as one that the government should use "a lot" for getting the revenue to fund government programs. No other tax we asked about—sales taxes, personal income taxes, property taxes, or payroll taxes—drew anywhere near as much support. Payroll taxes, which a plurality of Americans correctly see as paid more by lower-income earners, would be relied upon a lot by only 15 percent of the public— the *least* of any tax.

Another fact check: in the real world, U.S. tax revenue certainly does not come "a lot" from corporate income taxes. Because of growing loopholes and cuts in rates, the corporate income tax produced only 14.7 percent of all federal government revenue in 2007, well below the 30–40 percent level during World War II and the Korean War.[27] Instead, the government has relied more and more on regressive payroll taxes, which are used to finance social-insurance programs. Payroll taxes provide 35 to 40 percent of federal government revenue today, compared to 8–10 percent five or six decades ago.[28]

Tax policy greatly affects economic inequality. As the distribution of income has grown more and more highly concentrated, there remains even greater inequality in terms of wealth—stock holdings, mutual funds, retirement savings, ownership of property, and other assets. Chapter 1 showed that the top 1 percent of households have twice as big a share of wealth as they do of income.[29] Corporate income taxes and estate taxes are among the tools that other countries with private-enterprise systems and representative governance use to mitigate market-generated inequalities, including inequalities in wealth.

These are also tools that most Americans favor. But current U.S. tax policies do the opposite of what most Americans want. We rely heavily on payroll taxes, which working people disproportionately pay, but rely much less on corporation income taxes, which the owners of companies mostly pay, or on estate taxes, which moderate the inheritance of enormous amounts of wealth.

Recently some economists have challenged an old truth that seems self-evident: that the corporate income tax is paid by the (mostly affluent) owners of corporate stock, who get profits through dividends or capital gains. The theoretical argument is that—because it is now easy to move capital abroad—increases in corporate income taxes tend to drive economic activity overseas and thereby leave U.S. workers with lower wages, so that workers rather than owners end up paying part of the tax burden.[30] But empirical evidence on this is skimpy, and the magnitude of any such effect is unknown.

More troubling is that it has become harder to *collect* corporate income taxes, since accounting tricks can make corporate profits seem to be earned by subsidiaries in low-tax countries abroad, rather than at home, where they would be taxed. To the extent that corporate income taxes cannot be collected, Americans would seem to prefer that policy makers rely for revenue on other progressive taxes, not on regressive payroll taxes.

Despite the fog of technical complexity and misleading rhetoric, most Americans arrive at fairly sensible opinions about taxes that are more or less in harmony with their values and interests. Most support progressive taxation in general terms. Most perceive that certain taxes are more progressive than others, and most favor relying on taxes that they see as progressive. Moreover, majorities of Americans are willing to pay taxes to fund the social-spending programs they favor. They express willingness to pay *more* taxes for such programs.

Agreement on Taxes across Class and Party Lines

The spectacle of ferocious conflicts about taxes among politicians and pundits might create the impression that there are deep divisions in America between the parties and between high- and low-income earners. Despite the slugfest among elites and their warnings of "class war," the truth about the American public as a whole is dramatically different. The evidence demonstrates that majorities or pluralities of Democrats and Republicans, and of upper-, middle-, and low-income earners, mostly agree (repeat: *agree*) that taxes are necessary to fund essential government programs, that higher taxes should be accepted when needed, and that the better-off should pay more.

Deep breath. Such broad agreement among ordinary Americans contrasts so sharply with the in-your-face political theatre playing out in front of us that it may be hard to believe. Yet once again the evidence is overwhelming. It comes from our own Inequality Survey and from a number of independent, nonpartisan surveys by other experts.

For example, our survey makes clear that Americans across party and income groupings support the use of tax dollars for a number of government programs that expand opportunity and enable its exercise. Figure 4.4 shows that very large majorities of Republicans and high-income earners—up to seven or eight out of ten of them—favor using their tax dollars to help pay for early-childhood education, for job retraining, and for assistance to the poor. (Majority agreement also extends across races as well as classes.)[31] The number of Republicans and high-income Americans supporting these uses of taxes is just about as high as for defense and military programs, and much higher than for public broadcasting and the arts or for economic aid to other countries.

Solid majorities of Republicans and of high-income Americans break sharply with Washington politicians and pundits who claim to speak for them, even on some "hot-button" policy issues. Over 60 percent of Republicans and of the affluent support the use of tax dollars to provide welfare benefits to children of single teenage mothers. And more than half of Republicans and the affluent favor

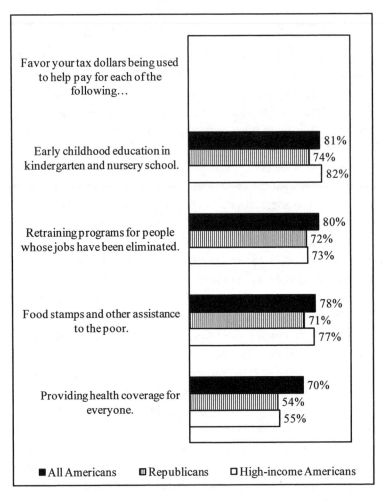

Favor your tax dollars being used to help pay for each of the following…

Early childhood education in kindergarten and nursery school.
- 81%
- 74%
- 82%

Retraining programs for people whose jobs have been eliminated.
- 80%
- 72%
- 73%

Food stamps and other assistance to the poor.
- 78%
- 71%
- 77%

Providing health coverage for everyone.
- 70%
- 54%
- 55%

■ All Americans   ⊞ Republicans   ☐ High-income Americans

FIGURE 4.4 Agreement across parties and classes on using tax dollars for concrete government programs. Source: Inequality Survey.

using their tax dollars to help fund health-insurance coverage for everyone.

Who, exactly, are the anti-tax zealots speaking for? Not for rank-and-file Republicans. Not for the top quarter of U.S. income earners, let alone for those in the middle or on the bottom of the income distribution.

Contrary to vehement "class war" rhetoric, there is also quite a lot of agreement across parties and classes about taxing the better-off. Figure 4.5 reveals that a majority of the affluent (though only a large minority of Republicans) believe that the government should "redistribute wealth by heavy taxes on the rich." About half of both groups sign on to the core idea of progressive taxes—that people with higher incomes should pay a larger share of their incomes in taxes than those with low incomes. Again, anti-taxers are not speaking for ordinary Republicans or most of the affluent.

Anti-tax advocates are also out of touch with the ordinary Americans who supposedly constitute their base when it comes to increasing taxes for specific government programs. Figure 4.6 shows that solid majorities of Republicans and of the affluent are willing to pay *more* taxes for kindergarten and nursery schools, and that close to half of the affluent and the GOP rank and file favor increased taxes for universal health insurance.

The mania to cut taxes reveals a wide gulf between anti-tax advocates and the folks in the country they claim to represent. Only 30 percent of Republicans and 30 percent of the affluent support

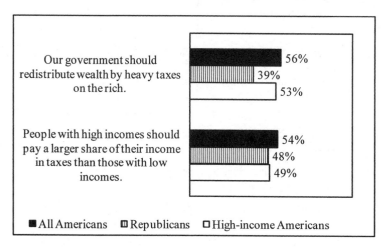

FIGURE 4.5 Americans, including many Republicans and those with high incomes, accept progressive taxation. Source: Inequality Survey.

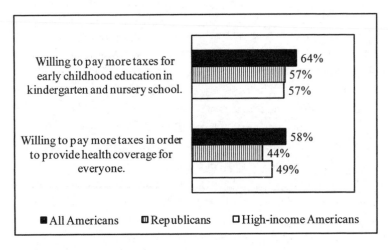

FIGURE 4.6 Americans, including many Republicans and those with high incomes, are willing to pay more taxes. Source: Inequality Survey.

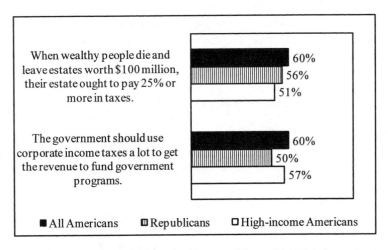

FIGURE 4.7 Americans, including Republicans and those with high incomes, favor estate tax and corporate income tax. Source: Inequality Survey.

"decreased" taxes in general, while majorities favor keeping taxes at the same level or increasing them. As figure 4.7 shows, solid parallel majorities also oppose zeroing out the estate tax, supporting instead a tax rate of 25 percent or more on estates worth $100 million.

Broad cross-class and cross-party support for estate taxes is echoed in support for another significant progressive tax—the corporate income tax. Majorities of Republicans and of the affluent agree that we should rely a lot on corporate income taxes. There is also convergence in preferring that the government use this progressive tax rather than regressive payroll taxes.

Even if our public officials ignored the millions of Democrats and independents and lower-or middle-income Americans altogether, if they simply responded to the wishes of Republicans and the upper quarter of our income earners, U.S. tax policy would provide money to strengthen opportunity and expand economic security for Americans from all walks of life. The effect would be to reduce economic inequality.

The Pragmatic Way—Paying the Bills

Other things being equal, most people would—of course—prefer to pay less in taxes. But other things are not equal, and most Americans know it. Most people from across our diverse society know that tax revenues are necessary to pay for the government spending programs they favor.

Some politicians and pundits work hard to treat taxes in isolation, to divorce them from the government programs they fund. Some pretend that taxes can be cut without harm by eliminating unspecified "waste." Some "charlatans and cranks" (as Jonathan Chait calls them) even claim that cutting taxes would *increase* government revenue.[32]

Most Americans see through the fiction that lower taxes are compatible with needed government action on education, health care, and national security.

The mystery is how politicians can get away with tax policies that are so out of harmony with the wishes of the American public.

5

Will Policy Makers Respond?

The evidence is clear. It contrasts sharply with the cartoonish pictures of Americans' thinking that are sometimes peddled by pundits and politicians.

Ordinary Americans are *not* ignorant of the extreme inequality of income and wealth in the United States. They are not indifferent to the enormous, widening gaps between the super-rich and everyone else. They do not reject government action to deal with those gaps. They are not tax haters, unwilling to pay the bill for egalitarian programs.

Warnings that public discussion of the increasingly lopsided distribution of income and wealth will ignite a ferocious "class war" are unfounded. Americans of all economic classes and both political parties largely *agree* with each other. We can talk honestly about economic inequality without fear that we will set off some sort of cataclysm.

Abundant evidence from our Inequality Survey and from decades' worth of other polls and surveys shows that most Americans are well aware of the extreme and rising inequality that has developed since the 1970s, generating spectacular gains for the super rich while stranding most Americans with a stagnating or declining share of the economic pie.

Americans are not happy about this. Most want income and wealth to be more evenly distributed.

Large majorities of Americans from both parties and from all income levels favor a wide range of government programs that would reduce economic inequality by expanding opportunity and providing economic security. They favor programs to ensure that everyone can get a high-quality education from preschool through college; that everyone who is able to work can find a job and get paid decent wages; that everyone is covered by health insurance, so that their chances to pursue the American Dream are not ruined by disease or injury; that seniors, after a lifetime of work, can retire with respectable pensions; and that those who are left behind through no fault of their own are provided with the basic necessities of food, clothing, and shelter.

Majorities of Americans—majorities of Republicans, of Democrats, of high-income citizens and of low-income citizens—are willing to pay for these programs. They favor using their tax money for help with schools, jobs, wage supplements, old-age pensions, and aid to the poor. They are willing, if necessary, to pay *more* in taxes for such purposes. And they want the government to rely for its revenue on progressive rather than regressive taxes.

The American Majority: Conservative Egalitarians

How can Americans possibly hold such views, when we know that they also support a free-enterprise economic system, insist on individual responsibility and individual freedom, distrust politicians, scorn government waste and inefficiency, and complain that their taxes are too high? How can Americans reject the idea of a "nanny state" while simultaneously favoring a broad array of expensive government programs and expressing willingness to pay for them?

The answer, which seems to be a well-kept secret, is that most Americans are philosophical conservatives but also *pragmatic egali-*

tarians. They look to government for help in ensuring that everyone has genuine equal opportunity plus a measure of economic security with which to exercise that opportunity.

America's conservative egalitarianism involves blends or compromises among three pairs of inclinations that push in different directions: belief in individual self-reliance but dislike of extreme economic inequality; skepticism about government but pragmatic willingness to turn to government when needed; and hostility to taxes but realistic acceptance of the need for tax revenue.

Nearly all Americans believe deeply in the American Dream. They want themselves and their children to have a chance to study, work hard, and achieve great economic success. They believe in material incentives and economic rewards. They do not want to level all incomes or confiscate the gains of the rich. They accept substantial levels of economic inequality in order to create the possibility of spectacular successes and to sharpen motivations to work and achieve.

On economic matters, then, most Americans are philosophical conservatives.

Yet large majorities of Americans want *less* inequality of income and wealth than currently exists. Even though they underestimate the incomes of corporate CEOs, they believe that CEOs should be paid less than the salaries they are now believed to earn—while factory workers, sales clerks, small-business owners, and GP doctors should be paid more. Most Americans are aware that the top 1 percent of wealth owners in this country now hold about half of all the wealth. Most Americans say that income and wealth should be more evenly distributed. And these views are not confined to the lower-income people or liberal Democrats. Republicans and upper-income Americans largely agree.

Americans' philosophical conservatism extends to a deep skepticism about government. For years majorities have said that the government wastes a lot of our tax money; that the politicians in Washington can't be trusted; that excessive government interference in the economy stifles growth and curtails individual freedom.

Yet an overwhelming majority of Americans want the federal government to spend "whatever is necessary" to ensure that all children can go to really good public schools. Large majorities want the government to make sure that everyone who wants to go to college can do so. They say that the government should guarantee that everyone can find a job, and that government should *provide* jobs if necessary. Large majorities of Americans favor raising the minimum wage and expanding the Earned Income Tax Credit, so that people who work hard will not be stuck in poverty. Large majorities favor a system of universal health insurance. Large majorities want to *expand*, not cut, Social Security, and want it to provide a decent income to retirees. Majorities of Americans say that government should make sure that no one goes without food, clothing, or shelter.

Again, these opinions are mostly shared by Republicans, Democrats, higher-income people, and lower-income people.

It is true that most Americans dislike paying taxes. For many years majorities have said that their own income taxes are too high. When polls ask about taxes in isolation from spending programs, majorities often say they favor tax cuts—especially when it sounds as if no programs will be curtailed and the tax cuts will benefit "all taxpayers."

Yet our Inequality Survey, which dug more deeply into tax attitudes than most previous surveys, revealed that there is *not* in fact a groundswell of sentiment for cutting taxes. When asked about tax levels in general, only a small minority favored lowering them; most want to keep them about the same. Asked to choose among a range of estate-tax rates on very large ($100 million) estates, only a very small minority of Americans—just 13 percent of them—picked a rate of zero. The average American favors an estate-tax rate of about 25 percent, a far cry from altogether abolishing the much-abused "death tax." Most Americans say the government should rely a lot on the taxes they see as progressive, like corporate income taxes, rather than on regressive measures like payroll taxes. To our surprise, a majority of Americans even say that our government should "redistribute wealth by heavy taxes on the rich," a sentiment that has grown markedly over the past seventy years.

We were careful to connect taxes with spending programs in our survey, just as the two are connected in the real world. When we did so, very large majorities said they favor spending their tax money on a wide range of programs that would expand opportunity, from early-childhood education to job retraining and health coverage for everyone, as well as provide some economic security through food stamps and other assistance to the poor and even welfare benefits to the children of single teenage mothers. Majorities also express willingness to pay *more* taxes for the two opportunity-expanding purposes we asked about: providing health coverage for everyone, and early-childhood education in kindergarten and nursery school.

How is it possible to reconcile Americans' preferences for such government programs with their philosophical conservatism?

The key, again, is that most Americans combine philosophical conservatism with operational liberalism. They are *conservative egalitarians.* They want opportunities for economic success and want individuals to take care of themselves when possible. But they also want *genuine opportunity* for themselves and others, and a measure of *economic security* to pursue opportunity and to insure themselves and their neighbors against disasters beyond their control.

Most Americans have a realistic view of the world. They know that childhood disadvantages like malnutrition or dangerous neighborhoods can be hard to overcome. They know that many of our schools are inadequate and that college is not always easy to afford. Americans know that good jobs are hard to find and can disappear in an instant as a result of turmoil on Wall Street or a business relocation overseas. They know that wages are often painfully low; that medical disaster can strike at any time; and that it can be difficult or impossible for millions of Americans to accumulate enough personal savings to fund a decent retirement in old age.

Facing these real-world problems—which have worsened with global economic recession, layoffs, downsizing, stagnant wages, and lost benefits—most Americans recognize that only government action can provide a measure of equal opportunity and create the conditions to exercise that opportunity. Only government action can provide protection against the thunderbolts of disease or injury, job loss, and other threats that can strike down individuals who are seeking to make it on their own. Only government can insure against unpredictable disasters and guarantee a floor or minimal level of food, clothing, and shelter.

When government action fosters genuine opportunity, individuals from a wider range of backgrounds can pull themselves up. The result is less inequality of income and wealth. The 1950s, when Republican Dwight Eisenhower was president, began a two-decade era of expanded opportunity. New and old government programs with bipartisan support, like the G.I. Bill and other educational and health-care initiatives, contributed to higher rates of real family-income growth for middle- and lower-income workers than for the most affluent. Measures of inequality declined or flattened out. The American economy was dynamic and grew vigorously.

To take seriously ordinary Americans' thinking about some of the biggest issues facing our country—inequality, the role of government, taxation—implies a high level of confidence in citizens' good sense. Some may find this confidence misplaced. In truth, one can certainly find examples of public confusion and error concerning such matters as the earnings of business executives or who shoulders the burden of personal income taxes. Nonetheless, the general accuracy of the public's perceptions is remarkable, given the complexity of government policy, deliberate efforts to sow confusion, and the wide range of topics there are to think about.

Indeed, our survey put people to a rather rigorous test by asking them to answer open-ended questions about wealth inequality, occupational earnings, and the like; they could not just "guess" among multiple-choice options. We were struck by how few Americans ducked our questions by refusing to answer, and by how close the collective responses came to objective realities. Despite wide gaps in individuals' knowledge, the American public as a whole displays notable skills in evaluating the world around us with the information at hand.[1]

Warnings about "class war" are nonsense. Although there certainly do exist differences of opinion, there is also wide agreement across income groups and partisan affiliations that inequality is too high and that government needs to play a role in expanding opportunity and economic security.

Given the sharp polarization of political elites in recent years, this agreement may seem surprising. It may seem especially surprising to see affluent Americans and Republicans agree that inequality is a problem, that government action is needed, and that it is appropriate to ask the most affluent Americans to "give back" more to support their society as a whole. But many or most affluent Americans apparently agree with Warren Buffett, Bill Gates, and other highly successful people that success results only partly from individual effort: it also depends critically on good luck—in having loving and economically advantaged parents; being born white and male in America; maybe being genetically "hardwired" for success; profiting from safe and nurturing communities; and having well-educated employees and coworkers, reliable infrastructure, and helpful government programs. Giving back makes sense.

Now that the views of affluent Americans and rank-and-file Republicans out in the country are plain to see, a question should be asked of politicians who oppose pragmatic steps to expand opportunity and security—For whom do you speak? Are you reflecting the actual opinions of those you claim to represent?

The absence of class war may seem surprising to those who wrongly assume that less-successful Americans feel bitter envy for the rich or want to seize their wealth and income. Being resiliently optimistic, in fact, most Americans vastly overestimate their own chances of getting rich. Ample evidence shows that even Democrats and lower-income workers harbor rather conservative views about free enterprise, the value of material incentives to motivate work, individual self-reliance, and a generalized suspicion of government waste and unresponsiveness.

We see no contradiction between Americans' philosophical conservatism and their pragmatic egalitarianism—or, to use the scary L word, their operational liberalism. A wide spectrum of Americans favor a kind of conservative egalitarianism that looks to individuals to make it on their own and supports government programs that foster opportunity and the conditions to pursue it.

But are enough politicians aware that Americans think this way? If not, why not? Can policy makers be persuaded to do what the American people want?

Why Does This Majority Seem to Be Silent?

Listening to partisan squabbling in Washington can make it very difficult to discern what ordinary Americans really think.

Many observers have failed to accurately size up public opinion, for at least three reasons. One is that Washington politics has been bifurcated into a latter- day war between the Hatfields and McCoys. Figure 5.1 shows that partisan polarization recently reached a level that is unprecedented over the past 130 years.[2] A one-sided presentation of Americans' philosophical conservatism is promoted by

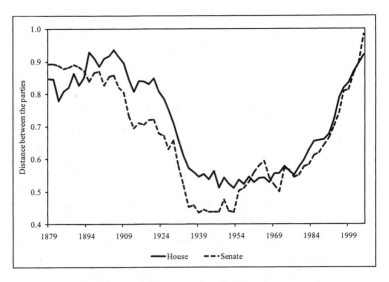

FIGURE 5.1 Polarization between political parties in U.S. House and U.S. Senate, 1879–2006. Source: Nolan McCarty, Keith T. Poole, and Howard Rosenthal, *Polarized America: The Dance of Ideology and Unequal Riches* (Cambridge, MA: MIT Press, 2006), at http://voteview.ucsd.edu/Polarized_America.htm.

the Hatfields, while the public's operational liberalism is touted by the McCoys. What's usually missing is a fuller picture of public thinking—Americans' conservative egalitarianism.

A second factor contributing to confusion among government officials and others about what Americans want is that the press tends to amplify political conflict. One rigorous study of fifteen years of press coverage of health-policy debates concluded that "the ebb and flow of political and policy developments have largely driven the decisions by journalists and editors over how to portray health care issues." Rising disagreement among government officials over Bill Clinton's health-reform initiative, for instance, led the "media [to] fram[e] their coverage in terms of conflict and gamesmanship."[3] The broader lesson is clear: the polarization of Washington elites over economic inequality and whether and how to respond to it has fuelled press coverage that conveys enormous discord. As if looking in the mirror, politicians and the press may mistakenly conclude that what they see is the country rather than their own reflections.

A third factor leading observers to miss the broad public support for measures to reduce economic inequality is a deep-seated assumption that human nature is fundamentally selfish. The framers of the country, generations of Americans, and many contemporary political and economic thinkers have all tended to assume that narrow, economic, individual self-interest predominates: that it explains all manner of behavior, including "pocketbook" decisions by voters to reward or punish incumbents seeking reelection. The assumption of self-interest leads naturally to the expectation that high-income earners and Republicans would overwhelmingly accept high levels of inequality, and that they would oppose government programs that would spend their tax dollars to ameliorate it.

Reality is quite different. Research on voting behavior, economic choices, and other decisions finds that individuals are motivated by a complex range of considerations. Economic self-interest is but one, and not uniformly the most important. For instance, careful analyses of voting find that citizens' evaluations of the national economy exert more influence on their decisions than just what is happening to their own pocketbooks.[4] A narrow and mistaken view of human behavior as singularly self-interested obscures the reality that most high-income people actually favor many pragmatic egalitarian programs, including fairly heavy taxes on themselves.

No wonder some policy makers are confused. But we should not let them off too easily. In a democracy, is it not the responsibility of political leaders to figure out—and pay attention to—the wishes of their citizenry?

If politicians fail to know or to heed what ordinary American citizens are thinking, when the political world is full of polls and surveys that can help them find out about it, why does this happen? Are politicians paying too much attention to special interests, to money givers, or to ideological extremists within their parties? If so, how can we get them to respond to what ordinary citizens want?

Will Policy Makers Respond?

Our main aim in this book has been to convey a full, clear, accurate picture of what ordinary Americans think about economic inequality. We hope that this book—along with the multitude of other opinion analyses that point toward similar conclusions—will demolish caricatures of the public's thinking, inform our neighbors about each other, and perhaps dissipate any sense of deep division or mutual suspicion that may currently prevail. We also hope to help inform policy makers about what Americans want and persuade them to respond by enacting the opportunity- and security-expanding policies that large majorities of Americans favor.

The 2008 elections raised some Americans' hopes for sweeping new policies that would reduce economic inequality. Actually, large majorities of Americans have favored some of these egalitarian policies for decades. Yet not much has happened. Republican and Democratic presidents have come and gone. Republican and Democratic Congresses have announced revolutions and then petered out. Hillary Clinton may have had a point when she proclaimed that "elite opinion is always on the side of doing things that really disadvantage the vast majority of Americans."[5]

If popular policies have been ignored or rejected for years, how can we expect success now? We believe there are reasons why policy makers may begin to pay more heed to the wishes of ordinary Americans. But before we get to this more hopeful future, we need to explain why politicians have not been listening in the past.

The American Revolution established a radical proposition—that "all men are created equal" and governments "deriv[e] their just powers from the consent of the governed." We enjoy a one-person, one-vote political system, and major social movements helped establish near-universal political rights that now extend to women, blacks, and almost all other citizens. The principle of political equality not only formed the core of America but also led the way for democratic movements around the world, starting with the French Revolution shortly after our Declaration of Independence.

Despite America's promise and its remarkable democratic accomplishments, however, our citizens do not in practice have equal voices in policy making. Some people have much louder political voices than others.[6] Substantial political inequality is built into our Constitution, our laws, our economy, and our society. For example, the Constitution prescribes highly unequal, state-based representation in the Senate. A single citizen in Wyoming has perhaps four hundred times as much clout in the Senate as does a single citizen of much more populous California. The numerous senators from small, rural states—who do not always represent even what their own constituents want—can block policies favored by the urban and suburban majorities of Americans.

The American system of governance is also loaded to produce stalemate and inaction. The system of separation of powers requires improbable agreement within and among two chambers of Congress, a president, and a Supreme Court. The difficulty of action is further compounded when different parties control the separate lawmaking branches. And the federal system divides powers between national and subnational governments.

But most important in thwarting egalitarian programs, we believe, is the great political power of *money givers, organized special interests,* and *unrepresentative party activists.*

Legally, each American has only one vote, but some Americans have lots more resources—such as money and organizational clout—than others do. Those fortunate Americans tend to get their way in politics, through campaign contributions, lobbying, public-relations blitzes, and heavy influence on political parties and elections. Some of the lucky Americans who get to cast multiple "votes"—including some but not all of our billionaires—are selfish enough to resist paying taxes and to resist government "interference" with the economy, even when government action is needed to help millions of other people.

We believe it is chiefly the political power of these money givers, special interests (particularly the owners and managers of large corporations and financial firms), and party activists that have repeatedly thwarted the will of ordinary Americans to enact conservative egalitarian programs.

Large and small businesses invest millions of dollars in advertising, consulting, electioneering, lawyering, think-tanking, and public relations. Their calculations are straightforward. They will get hefty financial returns on political investments if they can win contracts, subsidies, or tax breaks—or if they can block popular legislation that would raise their "labor costs" (i.e., their workers' wages) or their taxes.

Washington, D.C., and state capitals are filled with interest groups that act as hired guns to promote narrow sets of interests. Although citizen organizations exist, too, corporations and professional associations are far more extensively organized and well equipped with money, lawyers, lobbyists, and other resources. In the battle between special interests and ordinary citizens for the ears and the actions of government officials, victory often goes to the special interests.

The pull of party activists further tilts the playing field against the everyday citizen. After the "reforms" that followed the 1968 elections, control over the nomination of Democratic and Republican candidates shifted toward relatively small groups of activists within each major party. Many contests for congressional nominations, for example, are decided by small numbers of party loyalists who are intensely motivated by a few issues and who favor candidates that share their uncompromising and narrow policy goals. We know from surveys of presidential nominating conventions that the delegates often stand far from most Americans: Democratic delegates have been to the left of most Americans on social issues (but probably to the right on certain ecomic matters), while Republicans—especially in recent years—are much more conservative than everyday GOP voters or Americans as a whole.

Extremist party activists tend to choose highly ideological candidates, especially in "safe," one-party congressional districts. Moreover, the implication for officeholders is clear—crossing the party activists is likely to lead to a loss of campaign workers, costly and dangerous primary challenges by true believers, and a drop in campaign contributions.

Although Democratic officials might be expected to respond to ordinary Americans on economic issues, they, too, often rely heavily on vast contributions of money and talent from big-money interests, especially from investment bankers and from certain other multinational, capital-intensive firms. What the Democrats can or will do is constrained by their contributors' resistance to taxes, regulations, and other government policies that might raise their costs or impede their operations within the global environment of fierce competition.[7] Even the Obama campaign, with its broad Internet-based fundraising, relied heavily on Wall Street for early money.[8]

Neither Republican nor Democratic officials, therefore, can always be counted on to enact popular egalitarian policies. What can be done to encourage them to do so?

Pushing Politicians to Act

It would help increase responsiveness to the American public, of course, if our political system were thoroughly reformed to reduce political inequalities. Most of the relevant reforms are rather obvious.

Some of them would be extremely difficult to achieve, however. The separation of powers is untouchable. To get equal representation for all Americans in the U.S. Senate would require passing at least one and perhaps two constitutional amendments, a formidable task. To completely eliminate the power of money and organized interests in politics would be next to impossible. High-priced lawyers are very skillful at devising clever ways around any restrictions on campaign contributions, and Supreme Court rulings have called the giving of vast sums of money a form of protected "free speech." In the view of the current justices, those who can magnify their votes with money have a constitutional right to do so.

Other worthwhile reforms are more feasible. Proclaiming national holidays on election days and automatically registering all citizens to vote would greatly reduce the participation gap that currently disenfranchises many hard-working, lower-income citizens who cannot easily get away from their jobs in order to register and vote. Much more generous public financing of elections would dilute the effect of private campaign contributions. Then candidates could win without taking money from special interests. Outlawing the practice of drawing legislative district boundaries to provide a "lock" for one party's candidates would reduce the power of party activists to field extremist candidates who coast through general elections without facing genuine competition, and then hold office without any real prospect of being removed.

Many such reforms are doable. They are worth pursuing with energy and determination.

But the enactment of popular, pragmatically egalitarian programs need not wait for these reforms. It can be achieved, we believe, through what political scientist E. E. Schattschneider called the strategy of "expanding the scope of conflict."[9] Or, to put it more simply, *getting ordinary Americans involved, getting them organized, and making a ruckus.*

The first step is to make sure that the whole citizenry is aware of policy choices that would expand opportunity and economic security, and to make sure that politicians can unmistakably tell what the public wants. We hope this book helps a bit. Many actions can be useful—writing and speaking out in public; talking with friends and neighbors about the need for pragmatically egalitarian policies and for a more responsive government; contacting public officials by phone, letter, or email; attending meetings and congressional hearings; joining or organizing groups that push to ameliorate economic inequality.

The second step is to give politicians strong, self-interested motivations to heed the citizens. This requires exposing, loudly and publicly, the actions of officials who defy the citizenry. The major news media sometimes do a feeble job of this. They need prodding or supplanting, whether by journals of opinion, mass rallies, or blogs. To light a fire under officials requires an active, engaged body of citizens who insist on responsiveness, volunteer to work for helpful candidates, and punish at the polls any official who resists. Money talks, but politicians are also afraid of angry voters. Give them a whiff of possible electoral defeat and they are likely to respond.

Political activity and engagement are far from automatic for Americans. We have jobs and families, and we need time for recreation. Some of us have sunk into despair, doubting that politics can accomplish much good. Some have become shackled by resignation, disaffection, and hopelessness.

We say, throw off those shackles of resignation! Carve out a bit of time for politics. Stop letting politicians ignore your wishes. Take your political fate back into your own hands.

An aroused, active public can bring back what Abraham Lincoln talked about at that Gettysburg cemetery: "government of the people, by the people, and for the people." It can make great progress in moderating economic inequality and reviving the American Dream.

Appendix:
The Inequality Survey

Much of the data in this book come from the Inequality Survey of a representative sample of American adults, which was conducted for the authors in the summer of 2007.

The survey was conducted by telephone, between June 18 and July 8, by the Center for Survey Research and Analysis at the University of Connecticut (Samuel Best, director). The project coordinator was Chris Melchiorre, assisted by Chase H. Harrison. Interviews averaged approximately thirty minutes; the range was twenty to ninety minutes.

Respondents were selected by random digit dialing. The sampling frame was divided into four geographic regions: Northeast, North Central, South, and West. Quotas were set for these four areas based on population figures.

All data reported in the book are weighted. The sample component of the weight adjusts for differential probabilities of selection due to the number of adults in the household and the number of residential telephone lines which might have been included in the sample. Post-stratification weighting adjustments account for geography (census region), sex, age, level of educational attainment, Hispanic ethnicity, and race. Demographic characteristics were fitted using the iterative proportion fitting method. However, to improve the accuracy of overall estimates, sex, age, and education were entered in a single matrix. Since the sample was also proportionately stratified by geography, the impact of the geographic post-stratification adjustment was minimal but insured that other adjustments did not impact the stratification plan.

Because the sample was relatively small ($n = 608$), we can only be confident (at the p < .05 level) that estimates of population percentages around 50 percent are accurate to within about 4 percentage points. Very few of our findings are sensitive to this, however. On many of the issues we discuss, egalitarian policies were supported by 60 percent, 70 percent, or even 80 percent of those interviewed. Majorities of such magnitudes would be extremely unlikely to occur by chance due to sampling error.

We have not been able to report all the survey results in the book. For the full questionnaire and the marginal frequencies of all responses, as well as over-time trend data, see the publisher's website, http://www.press.uchicago.edu/books/page.

Notes

PREFACE

1. Alec MacGillis, "Obama Addresses Income Inequality," *Washington Post*, November 8, 2008, A6.
2. See Lawrence R. Jacobs and Theda Skocpol, *Inequality and American Democracy* (New York: Russell Sage Foundation, 2005).

CHAPTER ONE

1. John Edwards (speech in Charles City, Iowa, August 15, 2007). Accessed at http://johnedwards.com/media/video/iowa-tour-economic-inequality/.
2. Ben Bernanke, "The Level and Distribution of Economic Well-Being" (remarks before the Greater Omaha Chamber of Commerce, February 6, 2007). Accessed at http://federalreserve.gov.
3. George W. Bush, "State of the Economy" (speech delivered at Federal Hall, January 31, 2007).
4. http://www.templetons.com/brad/billg.html.
5. Louis Uchitelle, "The Richest of the Rich, Proud of a New Gilded Age," "Ages of Riches" series, *New York Times*, July 15, 2007, A1.

6. Roger Lowenstein, "The Inequality Conundrum," *New York Times Magazine*, June 10, 2007, 11–14; Uchitelle, "The Richest of the Rich"; Stephen Taub, "The Top 25 Moneymakers: The New Tycoons," *Alpha*, April 24, 2007.

7. World Bank Indicators Data Set. Accessed at http://siteresources.worldbank .org/DATASTATISTICS/Resources/GDP.pdf.

8. "Alpha's Top Moneymakers" *Alpha*, April 16, 2008. Accessed at http://www .alphamagazine.com/Article.aspx?ArticleID=1914971.

9. Data in this section based on Lawrence Mishel, Jared Bernstein, and Sylvia Allegretto, *State of Working America 2006/2007* (Ithaca: Cornell University Press, 2006); Lane Kenworthy, *Jobs with Equality* (New York: Oxford University Press, 2008.)

10. Mishel, Bernstein, and Allegretto, *State of Working America 2006/2007*, 6.

11. Ibid., 37,39.

12. Gary Rivlin, "The Millionaires Who Don't Feel Rich," *New York Times*, August 5, 2007, 1A.

13. Mishel, Bernstein, and Allegretto, *State of Working America 2006/2007*, table 1.2.

14. Thomas Piketty and Emmanuel Saez, "Income Inequality in the United States, 1913–1998," *Quarterly Journal of Economics* 118 (2003): 1–39; tables updated to 2006 at http://elsa.berkeley.edu/~saez/.

15. Mishel, Bernstein, and Allegretto, *State of Working America 2006/2007*, figure 1L. Accessed at http://www.stateofworkingamerica.org/tabfig/01/ SWA06_Fig1L.jpg.

16. Ibid., table 5.1.

17. In 2004 the top 1 percent of U.S. wealth holders held a remarkable 44.8 percent of all stocks and mutual funds and 63.8 percent of all financial securities. Edward N. Wolff, "Recent Trends in Household Wealth in the United States: Rising Debt and the Middle-Class Squeeze" (working paper 502, The Levy Economics Institute of Bard College, June 2007), 26.

18. Authors' calculations from Wojciech Kopczuk and Emmanuel Saez, "Top Wealth Shares in the United States, 1916–2000: Evidence from Estate Tax Returns," *National Tax Journal* 57 (June 2004, part 2): 445–87. Estate-tax data tend to understate wealth inequality because many assets of the very wealthy are dispersed before they show up on estate-tax returns.

19. Edward N. Wolff, *Top Heavy: The Increasing Inequality of Wealth in America and What Can Be Done about It*, exp. ed. (New York: The New Press, 2002).

20. Uchitelle, "The Richest of the Rich."

21. Mimi Swartz, "Shop Stewards on Fantasy Island," *New York Times Magazine*, June 10, 2007, 58–64.

22. Barbara Ehrenreich, *Nickel and Dimed: On (Not) Getting by in America* (New York: Holt, 2001).

23. David Brooks, "A Reality-Based Economy," *New York Times*, July 24, 2007, A23.

24. We are making two points: (1) The concept of inequality refers to dispersion or concentration in a distribution (measured by 90/10 ratios, Gini coefficients, and the like), rather than to central tendencies (measured by "averages," means, medians). (2) As to what is happening to the "average person," the *median* is a much better measure of central tendency than the mean, since the latter can be distorted by extreme outliers like Bill Gates.

25. William Kristol, "American Democracy in an Age of Rising Inequality," National Press Club, June 2004, CSPAN.

26. Alan Reynolds, "Has U.S. Income Inequality *Really* Increased?" (policy analysis no. 586, January 8, 2007). Accessed at http://www.cato.org/pub _display.php?pub_id=6880.

27. W. Michael Cox, "It's Not a Wage Gap but an Age Gap," *New York Times*, April 21, 1996, sec. 4, 15.

28. Mary Corcoran and Jordan Matsudaira, "Is It Getting Harder to Get Ahead? Cohort Differences in Economic Attainments in Early Adulthood," in *On the Frontier of Adulthood*, ed. Richard Settersten, Frank Furstenberg, and Rub´en Rumbaut (Chicago: University of Chicago Press, 2005), 356–95.

29. Katharine Bradbury and Jane Katz, "Women's Labor Market Involvement and Family Income Mobility When Marriages End," Federal Reserve Bank of Boston, *New England Economic Review* (2002 Q4): 41–74. A further point: temporary fluctuations in income may seem uninteresting or unimportant to afficionados of the "lifetime income" construct. But of course we live in the present. An expectation of respectable lifetime earnings (against which it is very difficult to borrow for current consumption) is little consolation to people who are temporarily out of work or otherwise distressed. Inequality at one point in time is real.

30. Mishel, Bernstein, and Allegretto, *State of Working America 2006/2007*, 3–4; Samuel Bowles, Herbert Gintis, and Melissa Osborne Groves, eds., *Unequal Chances: Family Background and Economic Success* (Princeton: Princeton University Press, 2005); Peter Gottschalk, "Inequality, Income Growth, and Mobility: The Basic Facts," *Journal of Economic Perspectives* 11 (1997): 21–40.

31. Timothy Smeeding, "Public Policy, Economic Inequality, and Poverty: The US in Comparative Perspective," *Social Science Quarterly* 86, no. 1 (December

2005): 955–83. Stephen L. Morgan, David B. Grusky, and Gary S. Fields, eds., *Mobility and Inequality: Frontiers of Research in Sociology and Economics* (Stanford: Stanford University Press, 2006). Miles Corak, ed., *Generational Income Mobility in North America and Europe* (New York: Cambridge University Press, 2004) indicates that economic mobility is very similar in Germany and the U.S. Results for the UK vary according to the data used (NLS shows much higher average mobility in the U.S., but PSID indicates similar rates in both countries; see chap. 5, esp. 70–79). Bernanke, "The Level and Distribution of Economic Well-Being."

32. David Brooks, "Truck Stop Confidential," *New York Times*, August 14, 2007, A21.

33. Bush, "State of the Economy" (January 31, 2007).

34. Bernanke, "The Level and Distribution of Economic Well-Being."

35. Uchitelle, "The Richest of the Rich."

36. James Madison, paper 10 in *The Federalist Papers*, ed. Clinton Rossiter (New York: New American Library, 1961), 77–84.

37. George Will, "The Equality Engineer," *Washington Post*, January 21, 2007, B7.

38. George Will, "The Case for Conservatism," *Washington Post*, May 31, 2007, A19.

39. *Washington Post*, "The Politics of Inequality Have Shifted. Now Policy Must Follow," "Seize the Chance" series, December 24, 2006, B6.

40. Bernanke, "The Level and Distribution of Economic Well-Being."

41. Uchitelle, "The Richest of the Rich."

42. Jennifer Hochschild, *What's Fair? American Beliefs about Distributive Justice* (Cambridge: Harvard University Press, 1981). See especially page 1: "the American poor apparently do not support the downward redistribution of wealth."

43. Louis Hartz, *The Liberal Tradition in America: An Interpretation of American Political Thought Since the Revolution* (New York: Harcourt, Brace, 1955).

44. Brooks, "Truck Stop Confidential."

45. Ira Katznelson, *City Trenches: Urban Politics and the Patterning of Class in the United States* (New York: Pantheon Books, 1981). See also David Brody, *Workers in Industrial America: Essays on the Twentieth-Century Struggle*, 2nd ed. (New York: Oxford University Press, 1993).

46. Will, "The Case for Conservatism."

47. Brooks, "A Reality-Based Economy."

48. Bush, "State of the Economy" (January 31, 2007).

49. Bernanke, "The Level and Distribution of Economic Well-Being."

50. Larry Mishel, "Work Inequality and Stagnation: Skill or Power Shortage?"

(presented at the McCormick-Tribune conference on Economic Inequality and the Hourglass Economy, the Federal Reserve Bank of Chicago, April 2–3, 2008); James K. Galbraith, "American Economic Inequality: A Brief Tour of Some Facts" (luncheon keynote presentation at the McCormick-Tribune conference on Economic Inequality and the Hourglass Economy, the Federal Reserve Bank of Chicago, April 2–3, 2008).

51. *Washington Post*, "The Politics of Inequality Have Shifted."
52. Bernanke, "The Level and Distribution of Economic Well-Being."
53. *Washington Post*, "The Politics of Inequality Have Shifted."
54. Swartz, "Shop Stewards on Fantasy Island."
55. Uchitelle, "The Richest of the Rich."
56. Ibid.
57. Ibid.
58. Gary Rivlin, "The Millionaires Who Don't Feel Rich," *New York Times*, August 5, 2007, 1A.
59. Mishel, Bernstein, and Allegretto, *State of Working America 2006/2007*, chap. 8.
60. Lloyd A. Free and Hadley Cantril, *The Political Beliefs of Americans* (New York: Simon and Schuster, 1968).

CHAPTER TWO

1. The Inequality Survey was fielded by the Center for Survey Research and Analysis at the University of Connecticut. Interviews with a national sample of adults ($n = 608$) were conducted by telephone (RDD sample) between June 18 and July 8, 2007. All data reported here are weighted to ensure representativeness by region, sex, age, level of educational attainment, Hispanic ethnicity, and race. Estimates of population percentages are accurate to within about 4 percentage points at the $p < .05$ level.

For more details about the Inequality Survey, see the appendix. Full question wordings and marginal frequencies of responses, together with trend data from past surveys asking the same questions, are given at the University of Chicago Press website: http:// www.press.uchicago.edu/books/ page.

2. Adam Smith, *The Theory of Moral Sentiments* (London: A. Millar and A. Kincaid and J. Bell, 1759). See Lawrence Brown and Lawrence Jacobs, *The Private Abuse of the Public Interest* (Chicago: University of Chicago Press, 2008).

3. Robert J. Samuelson, "Who Cares How Rich Bill Gates Is?" *Washington Post*, May 2, 2001, A21.

4. http://en.wikipedia.org/wiki/Horatio_Alger; http://www.pbs.org/benfrank lin/l3_wit_self.html.
5. Samuel Popkin and Henry Kim, "It's Uphill for the Democrats," *Washington Post*, March 11, 2007, B1.
6. Michael Kanell, "Movin' on up? Economic Mobility Has Decreased since 1980," *Atlanta Journal-Constitution*, April 1, 2007, D1.
7. Janny Scott and David Leonhardt, "Class in America: Shadowy Lines That Still Divide," *New York Times*, May 15, 2005, 1.
8. Scott and Leonhardt, "Class in America."
9. Joseph Berger, "Some Wonder If Cash for Good Test Scores Is the Wrong Kind of Lesson," *New York Times*, August 8, 2007, B9.
10. Scott and Leonhardt, "Class in America." See http://www.forbes.com.
11. Mike Swift, "California's Income Gap: Silicon Valley Highfliers Grow Even Richer," *San Jose Mercury News*, June 24, 2007.
12. John Hinderaker and Scott Johnson, "The Truth about Income Inequality" (report of the Center of the American Experiment, December 1995).
13. Scott and Leonhardt, "Class in America."
14. Ibid.
15. Everett Carll Ladd and Karlyn H. Bowman, *Attitudes toward Economic Inequality* (Washington, D.C.: AEI Press, 1998) compiles a wealth of survey data up to the late 1990s. See chapter 2.
16. Ibid., 16–18.
17. Just over 16 percent said that in order to get people to work hard, large differences in pay are "absolutely" necessary; just over 41 percent said "probably" necessary.
18. Stanley Feldman and John Zaller, "The Political Culture of Ambivalence: Ideological Responses to the Welfare State," *American Journal of Political Science* 36 (February 1992): 268–307.
19. "Democrats" are the 35.1 percent of respondents in the Inequality Survey who said that, generally speaking, they usually thought of themselves as a Democrat rather than a Republican or an independent. Independents who thought of themselves as closer to the Democratic Party than to the Republicans are not included.
20. "Low-income earners" are the 27.5 percent of Inequality Survey respondents who reported that the total yearly income of all family members living at home was less than $40,000.
21. Leslie McCall, "Do They Know and Do They Care? Americans' Awareness of Rising Inequality" (unpublished manuscript, Northwestern University, 2005). See McCall, "Does Lack of Support for Redistributive Policies Imply

Tolerance for Inequality? Insights from the Era of Rising Inequality in the United States" (paper prepared for the meetings of the International Sociological Association, Durban, South Africa, July 2006).

22. For our questions about how much people in various occupations "ACTU-ALLY" [sic] earn and "SHOULD" [sic] earn, the order of occupations was randomly varied to avoid question-order effects.

23. None of our seven questions got more than 7 percent "don't know" or no-opinion answers. Similar questions on the 1987 and 2000 GSS surveys got only 11–14 percent "don't know" responses.

24. The median is the figure in the middle when all numbers are arranged in order. Its advantage over a mean (arithmetic average) is that it is not distorted by extremely high or low numbers, e.g., by one or two individuals who grossly overestimate the earnings of a particular occupation. In order to avoid the misleading implications of means, we use median figures for the public's perceptions throughout the book.

25. Paul Norton, *Madison (WI) Capital Times*, December 4, 1997, 1A.

26. Swift, "California's Income Gap."

27. GSS, "Joblose" series, 1977 to 2002.

28. Griff Witte, "As Income Gap Widens, Uncertainty Spreads," *Washington Post*, September 20, 2004, A1.

29. Samuel G. Freedman, "Getting into College," *New York Times*, June 6, 2007, B7.

30. Jim DeBrosse and William Hershey, "Area Workers Learn to Stretch Dollars Further in Ohio's Uneven Economy," *Dayton (OH) Daily News*, September 2, 2007, A12.

31. Ibid.

32. Earnings of production workers ($16,000) and machine operators ($20,000), http://simplyhired.com (accessed November 8, 2007). Of sales clerks ($26,000), http://indeed.com (accessed November 8, 2007). Of skilled factory workers ($44,000), http://simplyhired.com (November 8, 2007). Of shop owners ($60,000), http://simplyhired.com (accessed January 9, 2008). Earnings of practitioners of family medicine ($185,740), cardiac and thoracic surgeons ($460,000), 2007 AMGA survey at http://cejkasearch.com. Heart transplant surgeons median ($405,725), April 2007 HR survey by salary.com.

In the few cases in which official occupational categories are sufficiently comparable to those in our survey questions, government estimates of earnings are similar to those given above. For example, "precision production, craft and repair" workers (roughly comparable to "skilled factory workers") averaged $41,496 in earnings in 2005; "machine operators, assemblers, and inspectors" (roughly comparable to "unskilled factory workers") averaged $29,515. U.S. Census Bureau, *2008 Statistical Abstract*, table 624.

33. CEOs of S&P 500 companies had an average income of $14.78 million in 2006. Corporate Library survey reported at http://aflcio.org/corporatewatch/ paywatch. Ratios calculated by authors.

34. "CEO Compensation," forbes.com (May 3, 2007). Total 2007 compensation of specific executives in "CEO Compensation Scorecard" at http://online.wsj .com (accessed November 8, 2007).

35. Pew release (February 15, 2007), at http://people-press.org. Public perceptions of levels and trends in inequality are clearly imperfect. Lane Kenworthy and Leslie McCall, "Inequality, Public Opinion, and Redistribution" (unpublished paper, University of Arizona, November 12, 2006), using 1980–90 ISSP (including GSS) data for eight nations, found that actual increases in income inequality were only weakly tracked by perceived inequality.

36. Trump's cars were described at cherryflava.com, http://www.cherryflava .com/cherryflava/2005/06/trump_car.html (June 10, 2005).

37. Matthew Benjamin, "America Takes Notice of Gap in Incomes," *Houston Chronicle*, December 18, 2006, business section, 1.

38. Our open-ended survey question on wealth distribution: "Thinking about people's wealth, including the value of their homes, money in the bank, stocks and bonds and the like, roughly how much of the total wealth in the United States would you say is owned by the top 1 percent of richest people?" Percentage estimates were recorded. Median = 50.0; mean = 47.0; standard deviation = 28.5.

39. Swift, "California's Income Gap."

40. Matt Casey, "Is the Middle Class Losing Financial Ground?" *Hanover (PA) Evening Sun*, September 3, 2007.

41. Wealth owned by the top 1 percent was 38.5 percent of all net worth in 1995, 34.3 percent in 2004; 47.2 percent of non-home wealth in 1995, 42.2 percent in 2004. Edward N. Wolff, "Recent Trends in Household Wealth in the United States" (working paper 502, Levy Economics Institute of Bard College, June 2007), 11. See Wolff, *Top Heavy*.

42. Mishel, Bernstein, and Allegretto, *State of Working America 2006/7*, 251–57, relying on unpublished SCF data provided in 2006 by Edward Wolff. Wolff, "Recent Trends," 11, found a rise in wealth inequality from 1983 to 1995 but then (as of 2004) a decline to about the 1983 level. Wojciech Kopczuk and Emmanuel Saez, "Top Wealth Shares in the United States," *National Tax Journal* LVII 2–2 (June 2004): 457–58, found relative constancy since 1946, except for a drop in the 1970s that was reversed between 1982 and 1986.

More recently the trend may have been toward increased concentration of wealth.

43. Benjamin, "America Takes Notice of Gap in Incomes."

44. An October 2000 *Washington Post* data point is omitted from figure 2.2 due to a change in question wording. Dropping the word "today" apparently directed less attention to the relative prosperity of the moment and led to a sudden jump in "more even" responses.

    The figure indicates a fairly steady decline in concern about inequality during the prosperous 1990s, and then an increase in concern with the 2000–2001 recession and subsequent wage stagnation. See McCall, "Does Lack of Support for Redistributive Policies Imply Tolerance for Inequality?" 8, 17, for generally consistent GSS data from 1987, 1992, 1996, and 2000.

45. Given four options, 55.1 percent of our respondents described themselves as "middle class," 30.0 percent as "working class," 9.5 percent as "lower class," and just 3.8 percent as "upper class." Even among the upper class, 61 percent said income differences are "too large."

46. Republicans are the 27.5 percent in our survey who said that, generally speaking, they usually thought of themselves as Republicans. "Leaners"— independents who said they thought of themselves as closer to the Republican Party than to the Democratic Party—are not included.

47. High-income earners are the 25.2 percent of our respondents who reported family incomes of $80,000 or more per year.

48. Bernanke, "The Level and Distribution of Economic Well-Being"; Steven Greenhouse and David Leonhardt, "Real Wages Fail to Match a Rise in Productivity," *New York Times*, August 28, 2006, A1.

49. Greenhouse and Leonhardt, "Real Wages Fail to Match."

50. Majority sentiment that "money and wealth . . . should be more evenly distributed" cuts across lines of race as well as class; it encompasses large majorities of whites (65 percent), nonwhites (80 percent), and two groups that were sometimes labeled "conservative" in the 2008 Democratic primaries: low-income whites (80 percent) and unskilled white workers (79 percent). The same is true of feelings that "differences in income . . . are too large."

51. Scott and Leonhardt, "Class in America."

52. M. D. Kittle, "America's Income Gap Widens," *Dubuque (IA) Telegraph Herald*, April 15, 2007, A1.

53. Ibid.

54. Witte, "As Income Gap Widens, Uncertainty Spreads."

55. Ibid.

56. Casey, "Is the Middle Class Losing Financial Ground?"

CHAPTER THREE

1. Robert Dreyfuss, "Grover Norquist: 'Field Marshal' of the Bush Tax Plan," *Nation* 272, no. 19 (May 14, 2001): 11–16.

2. Proportions saying it is still possible to start out poor, work hard, and become rich: whites, 76 percent; nonwhites, 77 percent; low-income whites, 67 percent; unskilled white workers, 57 percent.

3. Samuel Bowles, Herbert Gintis, and Melissa Osborne Groves, eds., *Unequal Chances* (New York: Russell Sage, 2005), 2.

4. CBS/*New York Times*, January 1983, June 1983, April 1986, July 1988, February 1996, March 1996, April 1998, February 2000, July 2003, March 2005, June 2007, with some wording variations; Inequality Survey, June 2007. The lowest "still possible to . . . become rich" response (51 percent) came in 1986, amidst rapidly increasing inequality. The highest (84 percent) came in prosperous 2000.

5. Marjory Raymer, "Social Security Plan a Tough Sell; State of the Union," *Flint (MI) Journal*, February 3, 2005, A1.

6. Support for the proposition that "government must always protect private property": whites, 63 percent; nonwhites, 68 percent; low-income whites, 72 percent; unskilled white workers, 79 percent. Large majorities of all these groups also said that "our freedom depends on the free enterprise system" and that "the people in the government waste a lot of money we pay in taxes."

7. Hochschild, *What's Fair?* e.g., 161, 181–82, found similar reactions to her original open-ended version of the "protect property"/eminent domain question. Since this question (which we adopted from Hochschild) makes no mention of the "just compensation" guaranteed by the Fifth Amendment to the Constitution, it might be interpreted as referring to uncompensated takings. That very likely inflates the apparent opposition to eminent domain—perhaps especially among low-income and low-education people unaware of the Fifth Amendment guarantee.

8. Michael Abramowitz and Lori Montgomery, "Bush Addresses Income Inequality," *Washington Post*, February 1, 2007, A4.

9. 1958 PAB study: Herbert McClosky and John Zaller, *The American Ethos* (Cambridge, MA: Harvard University Press, 1984), 147.

10. Twenty NES surveys, 1958–2004.

11. In the Inequality Survey, 63 percent disagreed strongly or somewhat with the proposition that it is the government's responsibility to reduce income differences; only 36 percent agreed. With slightly varying introduc-

tions, an NPR/Kaiser/Harvard survey (February 3, 2005) found a 56 percent majority or 49 percent plurality *agreeing* that it is the government's responsibility. But all except one of nine surveys for the GSS, Kaiser, Harvard, and the *Washington Post* between 1987 and 2000—allowing "neither agree nor disagree" responses—found more Americans disagreeing than agreeing.

12. Ryan McQuighan, letter to the editor, *Baltimore Sun*, October 7, 2007, 16a.

13. Walt Jankowski, letter to the editor, *Herald News*, January 17, 2006, B7.

14. Sue Metzger, letter to the editor, *The Post and Courier*, May 8, 2006, A12.

15. Mark DeLuzio, letter to the editor, *Hartford Courant*, November 18, 2007, C2.

16. Michael Hoffman, letter to the editor, *Flint (MI) Journal*, October 22, 2007, A8.

17. Ibid.

18. John Legg, letter to the editor, *Tampa Tribune*, June 26, 2003, 2.

19. Laura Williams, "Wilkey Doesn't Fathom 'See You at the Pole,'" *Chattanooga Times Free Press*, October 6, 1999, B6.

20. Blair Erb, letter to the editor, *Syracuse (NY) Post-Standard*, July 29, 2004. The National Election Studies have tracked a major, long-term rise in agreement with the statement that "public officials don't care much what people like me think." In seven surveys between 1952 and 1970 solid majorities regularly disagreed, but the tide turned in 1972 or so. In all but three of sixteen NES surveys between 1974 and 2004, majorities agreed that public officials don't care. This was true even when (starting in 1988) "neither agree nor disagree" was given as an explicit option. In the 2007 Inequality Survey, using the dichotomous form of the question, 63 percent agreed and 34 percent disagreed that officials don't care.

21. David Brooks, "The Happiness Gap," *New York Times*, October 30, 2007, A27.

22. Hartz, *The Liberal Tradition in America*; Hochschild, *What's Fair?* e.g., 1; Ladd and Bowman, *Attitudes toward Economic Inequality*. But Hochschild, like ourselves, found general acceptance of specific egalitarian programs (183–84.) Ladd and Bowman did not devote much attention to specific programs but noted consistent support for a "wage floor" (104).

23. Jim Powell, *FDR's Folly: How Roosevelt and His New Deal Prolonged the Great Depression* (New York: Crown Forum, 2003).

24. Free and Cantril, *The Political Beliefs of Americans*.

25. Harris (September 1964), 57 percent "believed" in the statement about government provision of food, clothing, and shelter; PSRA for Pew (September–October 1997), 72 percent completely or mostly "agreed" with it; Inequality Survey (2007), 68 percent believed.

26. Matthew Winschel, letter to the editor, *St. Louis Post-Dispatch*, August 31, 2001, C16.
27. Frank R. Westie, "The American Dilemma: An Empirical Test," *American Sociological Review* 30, no. 4 (1965): 527–38.
28. Steven Greenhouse, "Clinton Seeks to Narrow a Growing Wage Gap," *New York Times*, December 13, 1993, D1.
29. By "high-income" or "affluent" Americans, we mean the 25.2 percent who reported annual pretax family incomes of $80,000 or more; "low-income" people are the 27.5 percent with incomes below $40,000.
30. Using the CCFR/CCGA format, we asked whether various federal government programs should be expanded, cut back, or kept about the same. Proportions favoring expansion were: aid to education, 74 percent; health care, 73 percent; Social Security, 55 percent; scientific research, 50 percent; defense spending, 29 percent; economic aid to other nations, 11 percent.
31. In 2007, only 8 percent of three-year-olds and 11 percent of four-year-olds were enrolled in Head Start: National Institute for Early Education Research, *The State of Preschool 2007*, 5. Available at http://nieer.org/yearbook/pdf/yearbook.pdf. As of 2000, only about three out of five children eligible for Head Start were in the program. Considering other types of federal children's programs as well, the situation is worse; the states served only about 14 percent of federally eligible children (approximately one out of seven) in 2000. Jennifer Mezey, Mark Greenberg, and Rachel Schumacher, "The Vast Majority of Federally-Eligible Children Did Not Receive Child Care Assistance in FY 2000," *Center for Law and Social Policy* (October 2, 2002): http://www.clasp.org/publications/1in7full.pdf.
32. In the fall of 2006, a respectable-looking 65.8 percent of high school graduates from the class of 2006 were enrolled in colleges or universities, according to the U.S. Department of Labor's Bureau of Labor Statistics: http://www.bls.gov/news.release/hsgec.nro.htm. But many do not make it to high school graduation. In October 2007, 21.1 million young people between the ages of sixteen and twenty-four, or just 56.2 percent of the sixteen- to twenty-four-year-old population, were either enrolled in high school (9.7 million) or in college (11.3 million).

    Bankrate.com commissioned GfK Roper to conduct a random survey of parents' college funding plans. "When asked to self-report, fewer than half of parents (47 percent) feel they can afford to send their kids to school." "College costs have soared with the average tuition at a public four-year university increasing more than 35 percent in the last five years and having more than doubled in the last two decades, after adjusting for inflation," says Tamara Draut, author of *Strapped: Why America's 20- and 30-Somethings Can't Get Ahead.* Cheryl Allebrand, "Half of Families Can't Afford College," Bankrate.com, http://www.bankrate.com/brm/news/Financial_Literacy/Sep07_college_poll_results_a1.asp?caret=60a (September 17, 2007).

The average Pell Grant covered 76 percent of tuition at four-year colleges and universities in 1990–91. Between 1991 and 2005, federal Pell Grant funding increased by 84 percent. But the average Pell Grant currently covers only 48 percent of tuition at these institutions. In *Measuring Up 2006*, the National Center for Public Policy and Higher Education assigned the forty-three failing grades. It calculated that from one-fifth to over 40 percent of annual family income was needed to pay college costs at public four-year institutions in some of the more progressive states in the country, including Oregon, Washington, New Jersey, Illinois, Ohio, and Iowa. Based on data from *Trends in Student Aid and Trends in College Pricing* (New York: College Board, 2005). See National Center for Public Policy and Higher Education, *Measuring Up 2006: The National Report Card On Higher Education*, http://measuringup.highereducation.org/_docs/2006/NationalReport_2006.pdf.

33. In the 2007 Inequality Survey, 49 percent agreed (strongly or somewhat) that "the government should provide a decent standard of living for the unemployed"; 48 percent disagreed. In 1987, allowing a "neither agree nor disagree" response, the GSS found 35 percent agreeing and 35 percent disagreeing.

34. NES, 1956, 1958, and 1960. Unfortunately this question was replaced in 1964, 1968, and subsequent years by a confusing query that mixed jobs and "a good standard of living." Americans react very differently to guaranteed jobs and guaranteed incomes.

35. PIPA, November 1999, December 2003, June 2005.

36. New econometric evidence and improved economic models of low-wage labor supply indicate that losses of very-low-productivity jobs due to the minimum wage are minor and are far outweighed by the direct and indirect gains in workers' wages. David Card and Alan Krueger, *Myth and Measurement: The New Economics of the Minimum Wage* (Princeton: Princeton University Press, 1995); see also epinet.org.

37. During ordinary times, some 8–10 percent of Americans have regularly worried that they are "very likely" or "fairly likely" to lose their jobs or be laid off in the next twelve months; the proportion has risen to 12–15 percent during recessions. GSS annual or semiannal "Joblose" series, 1977–2002.

38. United States Census Bureau, International Data Base (data for 2008), http://www.census.gov/ipc/www/idb/; UNICEF, *The State of the World's Children*

2006: Excluded and Invisible, http://www.unicef.org/sowco6/; World Health Organization, Statistical Information System (WHOSIS; data for 2008), http://www.who.int/whosis/en/index.html; James Morone and Lawrence R. Jacobs, eds., *Healthy, Wealthy, and Fair: Health Care and the Good Society* (New York: Oxford University Press, 2005), chap. 1.

39. Christopher J. L. Murray, Sandeep C. Kulkarni, Catherine Michaud, Niels Tomijima, Maria T. Bulzacchelli, Terrell J. Iandiorio, and Majid Ezzati, "Eight Americas: Investigating Mortality Disparities across Races, Counties, and Race-Counties in the United States," *PLoS Medicine* 3, no. 9 (September 12, 2006); U.S. Census Bureau, Population Division, Interim State Population Projections, 2005.

40. Congressional Budget Office, "How Many People Lack Health Insurance and For How Long?" (May 2008), http://www.cbo.gov/ftpdocs/42xx/doc4210/05-12-Uninsured.pdf.

41. James A. Morone, "American Sickness: Diagnosis and Cure," *openDemocracy,* October 16, 2007.

42. Paul Fronstin, "Sources of Health Insurance and Characteristics of the Uninsured: Analysis of the March 2007 Current Population Survey" (issue brief 310, Employee Benefits Research Institute, Washington, D.C., October 2007). Accessed at http://www.ebri.org/pdf/briefspdf/EBRI_IB_10-20073.pdf.

43. Americans in favor of expanding federal government health care, CCFR, 1994 (71 percent), 1998 (78 percent), 2002 (77 percent), 2004 (79 percent); Americans believing health care is the responsibility of federal government, CNN/USA Today, January 2000; Gallup, September 2000–November 2006.

44. CBS/*New York Times,* three surveys February 1980–April 1981 and seven surveys October 1990–December 1995; ICR for Harvard and RWJ, August 2000.

45. A July 2000 *Washington Post*/Kaiser/Harvard survey found that only 38 percent strongly or somewhat favored a "single government plan" for health insurance, while 59 percent opposed. In every one of seven surveys conducted for Kaiser/Harvard between 1998 and 2004, which offered a favor/oppose dichotomy, majorities (or in one case a plurality) opposed it.

46. PSRA for Kaiser and Harvard, December 1999; ICR for Kaiser and *News-Hour,* January–February 2000.

47. http://www.usatoday.com/news, November 3, 2007, 1.

48. Lawrence R. Jacobs, "1994 All Over Again? Public Opinion and Health Care," *New England Journal of Medicine* 358, no. 18 (May 1, 2008): 1881–83; Lawrence R. Jacobs, "The Medicare Approach: Political Choice and American Institutions," *Journal of Health Politics, Policy and Law* 32, no. 2 (April 2007): 159–86.

49. 1958 PAB study: McClosky and Zaller, *The American Ethos,* 271.

50. Fay Lomax Cook and Lawrence R. Jacobs, "Assessing Assumptions about Attitudes toward Social Security: Popular Claims Meet Hard Data," in *The Future of Social Insurance: Incremental Action or Fundamental Reform*, ed. Peter Edelman, Dallas Salisbury, and Pamela Larson (Washington, D.C.: Brookings Institution, 2002), 82–118.

51. Government Accounting Office, "Pension Plans: Characteristics of Persons on the Labor Force without Pension Coverage" (HEHS-00-131), August 30, 2000; Government Accounting Office, "Social Security Reform: Implications for Private Pensions" (HEHS-00-187), September 14, 2000.

52. Rebecca M. Blank, *It Takes a Nation*, (New York: Russell Sage, 1997), 20, 228.

53. JCPES, September 1998. Support among African Americans was 66 percent, a bit higher than among whites. Support stayed essentially the same in a November 2005 survey.

54. Americans in favor of expanding Social Security: CCFR, 1982–2004. See Cook and Jacobs, "Assessing Assumptions about Attitudes toward Social Security"; Lawrence R. Jacobs and Robert Y. Shapiro, "Is Washington Disconnected from Public Thinking about Social Security?" *The Public Perspective*, June/July 1998, 54–57; Lawrence R. Jacobs and Robert Y. Shapiro, "Myths and Misunderstandings about Public Opinion toward Social Security," in *Framing the Social Security Debate*, ed. R. Douglas Arnold, Michael Graetz, and Alicia Munnell (Washington, D.C.: Brookings Institution, 1998), 355–88.

55. Marjory Raymer, "Social Security Plan a Tough Sell."

56. Morton Parsons, letter to the editor, *Syracuse (NY) Post-Standard*, February 16, 2004.

57. John Alaria, letter to the editor, *Springfield (IL) State Journal-Register*, April 21, 2001, 8.

58. According to a 2005 report by the Social Security Advisory Board (which is required to use conservative economic projections), making all earnings covered by Social Security subject to the payroll tax beginning in 2006, but retaining the current limit for benefit computations would eliminate 115 percent of the seventy-five-year deficit. If benefits were paid on the additional earnings that were taxed, 95 percent of the seventy-five-year deficit would be eliminated. Social Security Advisory Board, "Social Security: Why Action Should Be Taken Soon," http://www.ssab.gov/documents/ WhyActionShouldbeTakenSoon.pdf, September 2005.

The new revenue that would be generated by raising or removing the payroll tax cap has risen rapidly as the incomes of the highest-paid Americans have soared.

59. In the Inequality Survey, after the payroll tax cap was described ("At present,

people do not have to pay any Social Security payroll taxes on money they earn beyond about $97,000"), 58 percent said "this amount should be raised, so that high income people pay more in taxes"; 33 percent said it should be kept about the same, and only 6 percent said it should be lowered.

60. Fay Cook, *Who Should Be Helped?* (Beverly Hills: Sage Publications, 1979). In May 1968 and December 1968, Gallup found 58 percent and 62 percent opposed to a guaranteed income of $3,200 a year for a family of four. In the same surveys, 78 percent favored a proposal to "guarantee enough WORK" to give a wage earner $3,200 a year.

61. Carmen DeNavas-Walt, Bernadette D. Proctor, and Jessica Smith, U.S. Census Bureau, "Current Population Reports, P60–233, Income, Poverty, and Health Insurance: Coverage in the United States: 2006" (Washington, D.C.: U.S. Government Printing Office, 2007).

62. Support for using one's own tax dollars to help pay for food stamps and other assistance to the poor: whites, 76 percent; nonwhites, 89 percent; low-income whites, 81 percent; unskilled white workers, 75 percent. This cross-racial support is especially striking because racial attitudes have been a potent source of opposition to welfare in the United States. See Martin Gilens, *Why Americans Hate Welfare* (Chicago: University of Chicago Press, 1999).

63. On many issues there are statistically significant differences between the views of Democrats and Republicans, and between the views of high- and low-income Americans. In a few cases (including certain aspects of health-care and/or tax policy) the differences are quite large, ranging as high as 30 or 35 percentage points. Yet even in most of these cases, *majorities* of the different groups agree with each other.

CHAPTER FOUR

1. *The Radio Factor* with Bill O'Reilly, May 20, 2004, from mediamatters.org.

2. Katherine M. Skiba, "Invoking Reagan, Armey Says Farewell," *Milwaukee Journal Sentinel*, December 7, 2002, 3A.

3. Jonathan Chait, *The Big Con: The True Story of How Washington Got Hoodwinked and Highjacked by Crackpot Economics* (Boston: Houghton Mifflin, 2007), 36. *Wall Street Journal*, "class-warfare" editorials, May 27, June 1, June 4, June 8, and July 6, 1993.

4. Michael Hoffman, letter to the editor, *Flint (MI) Journal*, October 22, 2007, A8.

5. Thirty-seven surveys between November 1968 and July 2007 by NES (18), CBS and/or *New York Times* (10), and others. Even in 1958 and 1964, when NES sur-

veys showed a more even balance between "a lot" and "some" waste, only 10 percent and 7 percent said "not very much."

6. Andrea Campbell, *How Americans Think about Taxes: Public Opinion and the American Fiscal State* (Princeton: Princeton University Press, forthcoming). Campbell shows that the ups and downs in "too high" responses reflect changes in effective tax rates and in the perceived benefits from government programs.

7. Philip Elliott, "Obama: American Dream Too Expensive, Taxes Too Difficult," Associated Press State & Local Wire, October 22, 2007; Michelle Singletary, "The Change That Hasn't Come," *Washington Post*, November 9, 2008, F1.

8. Rob Christensen, "Edwards Proposes Higher Taxes on Wealthy," *Raleigh (NC) News & Observer*, July 26, 2007, national political news section.

9. Kimberly Morgan, "Constricting the Welfare State: Tax Policy and the Political Movement against Government," in *Remaking America: Democracy and Public Policy in an Age of Inequality*, ed. Joe Soss, Suzanne Mettler, and Jacob Hacker (New York: Russell Sage, 2007), 27–50.

10. The Inequality Survey asked, "Next, I am going to read you a list of different kinds of taxes that governments collect. For each one, I would like you to tell me who you think pays a greater percentage of what they earn for these taxes, higher-income people or lower-income people."

11. We asked, "Thinking about the different kinds of taxes that governments collect, which sorts of taxes do you think are best to use for getting the revenue to fund government programs. Should the government use the following a lot, some, a little, or not at all?" For the income tax, only 15.5 percent said "a lot."

12. The proportion of U.S. economic output (or gross domestic product [GDP]) that goes to all federal, state, and local taxes is about 27 percent, compared with 34 percent in Canada, 37 percent in Britain, 41 percent in Italy, 44 percent in France, and 51 percent in Sweden. Figures for 2005, oecd.org.

13. ICR for NPR, Kaiser, and Harvard, February 2003; PSRA for Pew, June 2001; Gallup for Times Mirror, January 1989.

14. Suzanne Mettler and Matthew Guardino, "How Policy Information Influences Political Support for Tax Expenditures" (paper presented at the Midwest Political Science Association, April 3–6, 2008).

15. See Larry Bartels, "Homer Gets a Tax Cut: Inequality and Public Policy in the American Mind," *Perspectives on Politics* 3 (March 2005): 15–31; Larry Bartels, *Unequal Democracy: The Political Economy of the New Gilded Age* (Princeton: Princeton University Press, 2008).

16. Only 46 percent favored their tax dollars being used to help pay for "public broadcasting and the arts"; only 31 percent for "economic aid to other nations." The figure for "defense and military programs" was 77 percent.

17. Dan Judge, "One Challenged Seat in Napa Race," *Vallejo (CA) Times Herald*, October 17, 2006, local section; Mark Binker, "Parties Campaign for Control; The Democrats and Republicans Each Want a Majority on Guilford's Board of Commissioners," *Greensboro (NC) News & Record*, October 10, 2004, B1; Jeff Parrott, "John Glenn Expansion Plan Debated; Opponents Cite Rising Property Taxes, Declining Enrollment," *South Bend Tribune*, April 23, 2004, D1; Karen Adler, "Northside Hopes to go 4-for-4 with the Voters; $439 Million Bond Vote Set Saturday; 3 Previous Packages Have Passed," *San Antonio Express-News*, February 6, 2004, A1; Richard Roesler, "Eyman to Target Local Property Taxes; Ballot Measure to Call for 25 Percent Cut," *Spokane (WA) Spokesman Review*, December 31, 2003, A1.

18. Warren Buffett, interview with Lou Dobbs, June 19, 2005, at http://www.cnn.com/2005/US/05/10/buffett/index.html .

19. Bill Gates, Sr., and Chuck Collins, "We Still Need the Estate Tax," *Miami Herald*, December 26, 2006; transcript of Bill Moyers interview with Bill Gates, Sr., and Chuck Collins, January 17, 2003, at http://www.pbs.org/now/transcript/transcript_inheritance.html.

20. David Cay Johnston, "Dozens of Rich Americans Join in Fight to Retain the Estate Tax," *New York Times*, February 14, 2001, A1; Alison Fitzgerald and Ryan J. Donmoyer, "Buffett Says Estate Tax Repeal Would Benefit Richest," Bloomberg.com, November 14, 2007; http://www.responsiblewealth.org/estatetax/index.html, December 9, 2007.

21. W. Elliot Brownlee, *Federal Taxation in America: A Short History* (New York: Cambridge, 1996), chap. 2.

22. Randall Dodd, "Tax Breaks for Billionaires," Economic Policy Institute, policy memorandum 120, July 24, 2007.

23. GSS March 1987, March 2000.

24. Roper for *Fortune*, March 1939; Gallup for GM, April 1998; Gallup, April 2007; Inequality Survey, July 2007. This support was expressed despite the off-putting "heavy taxes" phrase and despite a slow-down-and-think warning: "People feel differently about how far a government should go. Here is a phrase which some people believe in and some don't. Do you think our government should or should not redistribute wealth by heavy taxes on the rich?"

25. Twenty-five percent was the *median* response, with equal numbers of re-

spondents picking higher and lower tax levels. Medians, unlike means, are not distorted by skewed or extreme responses.

26. Larry M. Bartels, "Unenlightened Self-Interest: The Strange Appeal of Estate-Tax Repeal," *The American Prospect*, May 17, 2004; Penn, Schoen, July 2005 and February 2006, at http://coalition4americaspriorities.com; (Luntz) BNA, "Estate Taxes Poll Shows 85% of Voters Favor Eliminating, Reducing Estate Tax," at http://policyandtaxationgroup.com.

27. United States Office of Management and Budget, *Budget of the United States, FY 2008*, http://www.gpoaccess.gov/usbudget/fy08, table 2.2; letter from CBO director Peter Orszag to Senator Kent Conrad, May 18, 2007, at http://cbo.gov.

28. *U.S. Budget FY 2008*, http://www.gpoaccess.gov/usbudget/fy08, table 2.2.

29. Mishel, Bernstein, and Allegretto, *The State of Working America 2006/2007*, table 5.1.

30. N. Gregory Mankiw, "The Problem with the Corporate Tax," *New York Times*, June 1, 2008, business section, 5; William C. Randolph, "International Burdens of the Corporate Income Tax" (Washington, D.C.: Congressional Budget Office, Working Paper series, August 2006). The standard "trickle-down" argument for cutting corporate taxes—that resulting economic growth will largely pay for the cuts and will raise wages—is valid only under special assumptions about what happens to government spending and/or other taxes in compensating for initial revenue losses.

31. Use of their own tax money to help pay for all the policies shown in figure 4.4 is favored by substantial majorities of whites, nonwhites, low-income whites, and unskilled white workers, as well as by middle- and upper-income earners and by both Republicans and Democrats. Low-income and unskilled whites—sometimes characterized as "conservative"—may tilt toward conservatism on social and cultural issues, but not on the tax or spending policies examined in this book.

32. Chait, *The Big Con*, chap. 1. Tax revenue could conceivably increase as a result of tax cuts if tax rates had been so high that the economy was grinding to a halt. But the United States has never come close to such a situation.

CHAPTER FIVE

1. For evidence on the consistency, coherence, and responsiveness to information of Americans' collective policy preferences, and for discussion of how this is possible in the face of low levels of factual knowledge, see Ben-

jamin I. Page and Robert Y. Shapiro, *The Rational Public: Fifty Years of Trends in Americans' Policy Preferences* (Chicago: University of Chicago Press, 1992); and Benjamin I. Page with Marshall M. Bouton, *The Foreign Policy Disconnect: What Americans Want from Our Leaders but Don't Get* (Chicago: University of Chicago Press, 2006).

2. Nolan McCarty, Keith Poole, and Howard Rosenthal at http://voteview.ucsd .edu/Polarized_America.htm.

3. Lawrence R. Jacobs and Robert Y. Shapiro, *Politicians Don't Pander: Public Opinion and the Loss of Democratic Responsiveness* (Chicago: University of Chicago Press, 2000), chaps. 5 and 6; W. Lance Bennett, "Toward a Theory of Press-State Relations in the United States," *Journal of Communications* 40 (Spring 1990): 103–25.

4. Jane Mansbridge, *Beyond Adversary Democracy* (Chicago: University of Chicago Press, 1980); Jane Mansbridge, "Self-Interest in Political Life," *Political Theory* 18 (February 1990): 132–53; Deborah Stone, *Policy Paradox and Political Reason* (Glenview, IL: Scott, Foresman, 1988).

5. Quoted in Patrick Healy and Jeff Zeleny, "In the Media Blitz," *New York Times,* May 5, 2008, A16.

6. Useful discussions of political inequality in the United States and its connections with economic inequality can be found in Lawrence R. Jacobs and Theda Skocpol, eds., *Inequality and American Democracy: What We Know and What We Need to Know* (New York: Russell Sage, 2005). See also Bartels, *Unequal Democracy.*

7. See Thomas Ferguson and Joel Rogers, *Right Turn: The Decline of the Democrats and the Future of American Politics* (New York: Hill and Wang, 1986). On the role of big-money interests even in the New Deal, see Thomas Ferguson, *Golden Rule* (Chicago: University of Chicago Press, 1995), and—for a slightly different view—Peter A. Swenson, *Capitalists against Markets* (New York: Oxford University Press, 2002).

8. Glenn R. Simpson and T. W. Farnam, "Goldman Hedges Political Bets: Executives Shelled Out for Clinton, Obama; Lesser Sums for GOP," *Wall Street Journal,* February 2, 2008, A6; Michael Luo and Christopher Drew, "Big Donors, Too, Have Seats at Obama Fund-Raising Table," *New York Times,* August 6, 2008, A1, A16.

9. E. E. Schattschneider, *The Semi-Sovereign People* (New York: Holt, Rinehart and Winston, 1960).

Index